This is my faith journey.

Invite the Holy Spirit into Your Life: Growing in Love, Joy, Peace, Patience, Kindness, Goodness,
Faithfulness, Gentleness, and Self-Control

Nihil obstat:
   Rev. Timothy Hall,
   Censor librorum
   September 15, 2018

Imprimatur:
   †Most Rev. John M. Quinn,
   Bishop of Winona
   September 15, 2018

24 23 22 21 20 19   2 3 4 5 6 7 8 9

Cover, interior design and composition by Laurie Nelson, Agápe Design Studios.

Graphic elements: © iStockphoto.com, © Adobe Stock

Copy editing by Karen Carter.

ISBN: 978-1-68192-501-1 (Inventory No. T2390)
LCCN: 2019939977

Stay Connected Journals for Catholic Women are published by Our Sunday Visitor Publishing Division, 200 Noll Plaza, Huntington, IN 46750; 1-800-348-2440; www.osv.com.

Acknowledgments

Scripture texts in this work are taken from the New American Bible, revised edition © 2010, 1991, 1986, 1970 Confraternity of Christian Doctrine, Washington, D.C. and are used by permission of the copyright owner. All Rights Reserved. No part of the New American Bible may be reproduced in any form without permission in writing from the copyright owner.

Quotes from the Catechism of the Catholic Church are taken from the English translation of the Catechism of the Catholic Church for the United States of America, 2nd ed. Copyright 1997 by United States Catholic Conference—Libreria Editrice Vaticana.

STAY
Connected
Journals for Catholic Women

Invite the Holy Spirit into Your Life

Growing in Love, Joy, Peace, Patience, Kindness, Goodness, Faithfulness, Gentleness, and Self-Control

Deanna G. Bartalini

Acknowledgments:

First, thanks to Allison Gingras, who reached out after being prompted by the Holy Spirit. Her yes, brought about my yes, all in answer to prayer. Our Lady, Undoer of Knots is with me always.

Thanks to Tiffany Walsh, for reading and suggesting and editing. I'd like to do this again with you!

Thanks to my husband, who may not have said yes to writing this book but who said yes to me writing it and encouraged me every step of the way. Reading it over and over and over; being ignored while I wrote; and believing in me. I am blessed.

Thanks to my friends, who think more highly of me than I do of myself.

And thanks, always, to our God and Father; may this be for his glory.

Opening Prayer:

Prayer of St. Augustine

Breathe in me, O Holy Spirit, that my thoughts may all be holy.

Act in me, O Holy Spirit, that my work, too, may be holy.

Draw my heart, O Holy Spirit, that I love but what is holy.

Strengthen me, O Holy Spirit, to defend all that is holy.

Guard me, then, O Holy Spirit, that I always may be holy.

Amen.

Table of Contents

Introduction: Cultivating the Fruits of the Holy Spirit 1

1: Joy 13

2: Peace 29

3: Patience 45

4: Faithfulness 61

5: Kindness and Goodness 77

6: Self-Control and Gentleness 93

7: Love 107

Introduction

Cultivating the Fruits of the Holy Spirit

Before we can begin talking about the fruits of the Spirit, there needs to be a brief explanation of the Holy Spirit. Who is the Holy Spirit? What does he do? Why is he important and necessary? Keep in mind that this introduction is not the definitive teaching on the Holy Spirit but rather a way to give our learning and discussion a frame of reference, to have some context, and to have a similar foundation as we dive into the fruits of the Holy Spirit.

God is Trinitarian—a unity, one God in three persons. The Father, Son, and Holy Spirit are distinct persons, each related to the other: the Father is related to the Son, the Son is related to the Father, and the Holy Spirit to both. And yet each of the three persons is God, whole and entire (see Catechism 252-255). Often people have more knowledge of the Father and Son, so it is good to learn more about the Holy Spirit.

Who is the Holy Spirit? Each time we bless ourselves, "In the name of the Father and of the Son and of the Holy Spirit. Amen," we invoke him as part of the Holy Trinity. In the Nicene Creed, we pray, "I believe in the Holy Spirit, the Lord, the giver of life, who proceeds from the Father and the Son, who with the Father and the Son is adored and glorified, who has spoken through the prophets." We celebrate the outpouring of the Holy Spirit at Pentecost, and remember it each time we pray the Glorious mysteries of the Rosary when we recall the "descent of the Holy Spirit."

Clearly, the Church thinks the Holy Spirit is important, but what about us? We may pray those words and prayers without ever having a connection with or understanding of the Holy Spirit. Do we need the Holy Spirit?

I think we do—and not only because the Church says so but because I have seen the power and necessity of the Holy Spirit time and again in my journey as a Catholic. As women of faith, who are searching for the best way to live out our faith, we need the Holy Spirit.

The *Catechism of the Catholic Church* tells us that the Holy Spirit reveals God and Christ to us, "We know him only in the movement by which he reveals the Word to us and disposes us to welcome him in faith. The Spirit of truth who 'unveils' Christ to us 'will not speak on his own.'" (*Catechism*, 687).

As I read those words, "reveals," "disposes," and "welcomes," I cannot help but think about women and how often we fulfill those roles in our daily lives. The Holy Spirit is necessary so that we can know the Father and the Son, so that we can have faith, and so that we can know truth.

This study will lead us to a deeper understanding of who the Holy Spirit is and how he acts in our lives, most especially through the fruits of the Holy Spirit.

Where Can We Find the Holy Spirit?

In the Old Testament, we find the Spirit present right from the beginning of Scripture, as "a mighty wind sweeping over the waters" (Genesis 1:2) and later, in the Garden of Eden, when Adam and Eve

"heard the sound of the LORD GOD walking about in the garden at the breezy time of the day" (Genesis 3:8).

Going further into Scripture, we find that the Spirit refers to strength and fortitude: "Send forth your spirit, they are created and you renew the face of the earth" (Psalm 104:30). In the book of Isaiah, "The spirit of the Lord shall rest upon him: a spirit of wisdom and of understanding, a spirit of counsel and of strength, a spirit of knowledge and of fear of the LORD" (Isaiah 11:2). Those are the gifts of the Holy Spirit, and the *Catechism of the Catholic Church* lists seven gifts of the Holy Spirit, wisdom, understanding, counsel, fortitude, knowledge, piety, and fear of the Lord (*Catechism,* 1831). These gifts are given to us in Baptism and strengthened in us when we receive the sacrament of Confirmation. We need these gifts because, as the *Catechism* says, "The moral life of Christians is sustained by the gifts of the Holy Spirit. These are permanent dispositions which make man docile in following the promptings of the Holy Spirit" (*Catechism,* 1830).

What Are the Fruits of the Spirit?

In St. Paul's letter to the Galatians, he talks about the importance of living for Christ, of holding firm in the faith, and that through our freedom in Christ, we can live by the Spirit. In chapter 5:18–26, he offers a contrast between those who live according to the flesh and those who live according to the Spirit. Read those verses and then write down the fruits St. Paul lists.

_____

_____

_____

_____

Citing this passage from Galatians, the *Catechism of the Catholic Church* lists these fruits of the Holy Spirit: love, joy, peace, patience, kindness, goodness, faithfulness, gentleness, self-control (*Catechism*, 736). The list we will use in this study is: joy (chapter 1), peace (chapter 2), patience (chapter 3), faithfulness (chapter 4), kindness and goodness (chapter 5), self-control and gentleness (chapter 6), and love (chapter 7).

We need these fruits to grow in holiness. Our lives are spent in the midst of an incredible amount of busyness, yet we often forget that the things we are devoting our time to are not always the most important things to focus on. Our focus, ideally, should be on becoming saints, which we do by working on getting into heaven. While that may seem like a very long-term goal (that's my hope anyway), it still can shape our daily life. Have we made sure to add heaven to our bucket lists?

In order to enter heaven and the presence of God, we need to be holy. Jesus reminds us, "So be perfect, just as your heavenly Father is perfect" (Matthew 5:48). This is not a demand for perfection but gentle call to strive for holiness in our lives.

Look at the list of fruits of the Holy Spirit that you noted. Stop and reflect a moment.

What fruits do you see in yourself? Which fruits do you need? How would having an abundance of the fruits of the Holy Spirit look in your daily life?

_____

_____

_____

_____

_____

_____

_____

_____

_____

_____

_____

_____

_____

_____

_____

An Abundance of Fruit

Let's answer that last question very seriously and together. Read Galatians 6:7–9.

What will you reap if you sow for your flesh?

_____

_____

_____

_____

_____

_____

_____

What will you reap if you sow for the Spirit?

_____

_____

_____

_____

_____

_____

_____

Which do you want?

_____

_____

_____

_____

_____

_____

_____

_____

_____

_____

I cannot answer for you, though I hope you can say with me that you want eternal life!

We spend so much time in life working toward goals. We also spend time waiting for one thing to happen so we can move on to the next thing. Goals are important and waiting is necessary, but are we setting goals and waiting for the things of the Spirit or of the flesh? Often a goal starts out as good and positive, but then it turns into an obsession.

For example, I enjoy entertaining. Give me a house full of people to feed, flowers, candles, and music, and I am in my element. However, when I was first married, my desire to entertain was a burden. I worried about every detail, badgered my husband to make sure the house was spotless, and I was not very pleasant to be around while preparing for company. My husband finally told me that while he didn't mind entertaining, my stress level before people came over was not worth it. Something had to change. I wanted to exhibit joy and generosity and goodness but, instead, was demonstrating the opposite, mostly to my husband, who was just trying to help and make me happy. I eventually changed my ways, and now we entertain without stress, but it took effort and prayer on my part.

Purpose of This Study

Spiritual growth takes awareness, prayer, effort, and a guide. The guide that we have for this study is the Holy Spirit. The foremost goal of this study is to help us become more aware of the fruits of the Spirit, to learn how to grow in them, and to discover how we can access them more readily. However, each of us will learn for ourselves what we need at this particular time in our lives. We will read Scripture, pray, discuss, and find our way to an abundance of the fruits of the Holy Spirit!

Go back to the list of fruits you wrote on pages 4–5. Look over the list and prayerfully consider which you have, which you need, and which you want. Write each fruit here in the most appropriate category.

Have	Need

Closing Prayer

Father, we give you praise for all the gifts you have given us: our life, our family, our friends, and our talents and abilities. We thank you for sending your Son Jesus to save us by dying on a cross for us. Our salvation came through his passion and death; our faith in the resurrection holds us up and reminds us, always, of your love for us. Thank you, too, for the Holy Spirit, who guides us in our daily lives, who breathes love, peace, joy, patience, self-control, faithfulness, goodness, kindness, and gentleness into our souls. Help us to turn to you, always, for all of our whole life is important to you. Speak your words into our hearts and minds, Father, so that we might know you more fully and trust you completely. Amen.

1: Joy

Opening Prayer

O Lord, fill me with your Holy Spirit. Infuse my soul with the joy of knowing you, loving you, and being your child. Slow me down. Help me pause. Give me eyes to notice all the joy in my life.

I desire to see the joy that permeates the world all around me, especially in the faces of the people I love and serve. Secure in me the hope that a life lived in joy pleases you, and take from me the things that prevent me from being joyful. I ask the Holy Spirit to fill my mind and heart with joy and to give me the courage to live out that joy in times of trouble.

Help my joy to come from you and not the fleeting things of the world. I want to share your joy with others. Let everyone I meet see the joy you have given me and be drawn closer to you. What you have for me is so much more than I can ever imagine, so I empty myself in order to be filled with all you have for me. Thank you!

Amen.

On My Heart

_____

_____

_____

_____

_____

_____

_____

_____

_____

_____

_____

_____

_____

Cultivate Joy with the Holy Spirit

How great is our God and Father that he wants the absolute best for us, including joy! This fruit of the Spirit, the joy that Scripture speaks about and that we can see in many people, often seems to transcend the harsh realities of life.

In Psalm 1:1-2 we see the way to have joy: "Blessed is the man who does not walk in the counsel of the wicked, nor stand in the way of sinners, nor sit in company with scoffers. Rather the law of the LORD is his joy; and on his law he meditates day and night." Clearly, the company we keep is either going to help or hinder us. And what else about ourselves might be preventing us from attaining that joy? What we think about needs to change.

Mother Teresa, now St. Teresa of Calcutta, is one person who comes to mind when I think of someone who has joy. If you searched for photos of her, you would see images of a woman filled with joy. It appears in her eyes, in the way she carried herself, and in the way she spoke.

Mother Teresa was a Catholic sister, now a saint, who served the poorest of the poor throughout the whole world. She founded the Missionaries of Charity, an order that now includes sisters, brothers, and priests as well as lay coworkers. She began her ministry in India, but her work and the order has spread all over the world to serve those in poverty.

I think that by her words "Joy is prayer; joy is strength: joy is love; joy is a net of love by which you can catch souls," St. Teresa of Calcutta gives us a starting point to understand what joy is and why we need it.[1] She knew where true joy comes from; it comes from God. Joy certainly encompasses more than happiness and contentment. Happiness is often based on what is happening at the moment, not on what is lasting.

With Whom Do We Associate With?

If we go back to Psalm 1:1-2, we are clearly told to not walk with the wicked, sinners, or scoffers. This is good advice overall; however, avoiding people who are not good company is probably easier than actually finding and cultivating relationships with people who will help us on our Christian walk.

Most of us have different groups with whom we associate. Oftentimes those groups are formed without our input, such as at work, at school, around activities for children, with our neighbors, and even with our family of origin. Some of these groups are constant, like our family, while others change depending on the season of our life. In some cases, we become friends with people from a group we find ourselves in. As adults, making new friends can be difficult. Sitting next to someone at a Little League game provides an opportunity to gain some insight into who that person is, but maybe not enough to decide if we want a true friendship with her.

I have been truly blessed with great friends in my life. Some have been a part of my life for so long that I need to stop and think when someone asks how long we've known each other. We have seen and supported each other through all types of joyful and difficult life events—births, marriages, new friendships, sicknesses, and deaths. All but a handful of my friends, I met in church. I should point out that I have worked in various parishes for over twenty years; spending a lot of time in church means you meet many, many people there! All of them have been given to me by God to love. We are not perfect; we have our struggles with jobs, children, husbands, aging parents, and health. Our common values draw us together, and we know that when we offer comfort or advice or opinion, it is given with our shared faith in mind. We keep each other focused on what is right, not on what is easy. We can offer a faith-filled perspective rather than the secular perspective of the popular culture. And, of course, we pray for each other.

Try, as much as possible, to associate with and surround yourself with people who share your values. All of your friends do not need to profess the same faith, but they should be people who strive to live a life that is in line with how you want to live your life. If you are unsure of where to start, maybe look around the table at the women with whom you are sharing this study; there is probably at least one person who needs you in her life.

What Are We Thinking About?

Each day we make choices about what to wear, eat, read, watch, and activities to participate in, and often without much thought. If we want to live with joy, many of us need to make a conscious decision to do so. In order to learn to intentionally choose joy, it can help to find out what causes us to feel unhappy or unfulfilled.

Our focus here is to move from a worldly perspective to one where God is first. In my own life, I did not experience this growing up. The main place a lack of joy manifested itself in my life was in always worrying about what others were thinking about me and comparing myself to those same people. The thought of joy never entered my mind. I worried and compared and always fell short. Always, in all ways, I fell short. It was a terrible way to live. I continued like this for well beyond my teen and young adult years. Even after I had a family, a home, and a career, there was very little joy. I was constantly chasing the next accolade. My need to do better than the other person made me difficult to work with at times, but somehow I was able to advance in my profession.

By the time I was thirty, I thought I had it all together—a great job, adorable and smart children, a house, and a husband who did laundry. From the outside, I was living an enviable life, but inside I was miserable. My work involved travel and many nights away from home. One month I had to spend more time away than at home. One night, during my usual phone call to my family, my daughter was very chatty, and she let me know that her brother was feeling better after daddy took him to the doctor. My husband and son had decided not to mention this to me so I wouldn't worry. I was upset that my son was sick, and I began to realize that I was missing too much. When I returned home, I started questioning the priorities in my life. After much prayer with God and talking with my husband, we decided that I would leave my job. It was not easy, but it was the right decision. I was able to find another good job in my field that kept me close to home. It was a major change but one that helped me to focus on my family in a way that had not been possible before.

This shift in priorities was necessary for my soul, my marriage, and my children, and it allowed me to have joy because I knew I was living the way God wanted me to live. My need to compare myself to others started to fade, and I was able to see my value as God's daughter rather than the sum of the things the world valued in me. While that was a major turning point in my life, I still had a long way to go.

What Causes a Lack of Joy

In addition to the worry that can consume us, a lack of joy can be tied to a lack of gratitude. When I speak of gratitude, I am talking about appreciating everything we have in our lives. From water to a roof over our heads to clothes to family and friends to our faith in Jesus, we have much to be grateful for on a regular basis. But are we? Is it possible that we forget to notice all the good in our lives? I often do. One reason for me is affluence. I work in a geographic area synonymous with affluence. And while my life is comfortable, I still have to do many mundane things like laundry and house cleaning and yard work. I often look over at the folks who do not, and I get a bit envious. It is funny that when I look at their Tesla, Audi, or Mercedes Benz, I'm not impressed at all. I'm envious of the time money can buy not the things money can buy, but that is still envy that steals my joy!

A habit that can cause a lack of joy is thinking that others' lives are better, easier, more interesting, or more fulfilling than ours. We live in a time in which looking at others through the lens of social media only highlights the great life all our friends are living, while we sit at home and fall asleep on the couch watching TV on Saturday night. Theodore Roosevelt said, "Comparison is the thief of joy," and I agree. When we live a life that is authentic and true to our values and goals, we don't need to compare. Instead, we can again return to gratitude. And remember, no matter how perfect a life may appear on social media, we all have struggles.

How to Obtain Joy

Many years ago my pastor gave a homily on joy. he used the word "joy" as an acronym for "Jesus, others, you," the idea being that we must put Jesus first, others next, and ourselves last. This makes sense. I know that when I spend too much thinking about my life, my plans, my problems, and whatever else is on my mind, I get bogged down in it all, and I feel overwhelmed and anxious—not very joyful at all. But when I turn the focus away from myself, turn to Jesus, and then take care of what he wants and needs me to take care of, life is better. It is not to say that I am unimportant, or that my needs are not worthy of my time and effort. Putting Jesus first helps put life and all of our efforts into perspective. It means that instead of asking God, "Are you okay with this?" asking "What's the plan?" and then following through with his plan.

An Invitation to Ponder

I have mentioned a few things that can steal my joy if I allow them to move unchecked in my soul, such as feeling like I do not measure up, envy, and comparison. I know they are interrelated and that sometimes one can lead to another. What steals your joy?

_____

_____

_____

_____

_____

_____

_____

_____

_____

_____

_____

Connecting to Scripture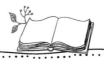

Take time to read each Scripture passage referenced below (and in each of the subsequent chapters), and pay special attention to what the Holy Spirit is calling your attention to in each verse. Do not concern yourself with right or wrong responses; simply relax and allow yourself to truly enjoy this time with the Word of God. Be assured, Jesus has no expectations for your time together; there is no perfect rubric for your time with Jesus, whether you are in prayer, reading Scriptures, or participating in the sacraments. The beauty of the *Stay*

Connected faith-sharing series[2] is that the time you spend with these books is your prayer time. Each of these journals is designed to be a guide for a personal encounter with the Triune God—Father, Son, and Holy Spirit.

If you wish, read each verse a few times, asking the Holy Spirit to guide your heart and mind to receive what he has prepared just for you. Use the space provided under each Scripture verse to note any inspirations or thoughts that come to you as you read. Share your thoughts with a small group or maintain your notes as a personal reflection.

PRAYER BEFORE READING SCRIPTURE

Father, fill me with the Holy Spirit to guide me as I read and reflect on your Word. I ask for the grace to allow your Word to flood my soul so that I may grow ever closer to you and your Son, Jesus. Amen.

Let us turn now to verses that will help us do as Psalm 1 instructs, to meditate on God's law and his Word and learn how God wants to give us joy.

🗲 Ecclesiastes 2:24–26 _____

_____

_____

🗲 Sirach 1:12 _____

_____

_____

❧ John 16:16–24 _____

_____

_____

❧ Philippians 2:17–18 _____

_____

_____

❧ James 1:2–4 _____

_____

_____

Scripture Reflection

It can seem that joy, or being joyful, is hard to attain and sustain. Life is full of reasons to not be full of joy. God knows this and wants to help us. Psalm 94 asks when will the wicked people stop gaining glory and understand who God is? It then goes on to remind us that those who are guided by God are blessed, are given rest, and will not be forsaken; the Lord's mercy holds us up. My favorite verse is Psalm 94:19, "When cares increase within me, your comfort gives me joy." God is ready to comfort us; he wants to comfort us. Proverbs 12:25

says, "Worry weighs down the heart, but a kind word gives it joy." There are many kind words from God that we have read that can give us joy. We can know these words by staying close to him as we saw in Ecclesiastes 2:24–26. Stay with God, especially in his Word, which is ours to read, to learn, and to pray over.

I fight against being negative on a regular basis. So, when I read those verses, I recall that my joy does not come from the world. It cannot be dependent on the day or the activity or the weather or a person. All of those things can change in an instant and can take away whatever I think was bringing me joy. True joy comes from being in tune with God.

We can have joy because God has given us comfort, mercy, protection, and salvation. Consider Psalm 63:8: "You are indeed my savior, and in the shadow of your wings I shout for joy." When life threatens to over-whelm us, run to the shadow of his wings and be loved. The knowl-edge of that love is what gives us joy. Sirach reminds us that fear of the Lord gives us joy. Fear of the Lord is not being afraid of God; rather, it is knowing that God is God, and you are not. It is remembering the natural order of things: we are the created, and not the Creator.

Jesus reminds us in John 16:16–24 that all of our trials, our grief, our mourning, and our weeping will turn to joy when he is with us. And while we are waiting for him to come again, he is with us now, most perfectly in the Eucharist but also in Scripture. James acknowledges our trials of life, but he tells us to consider them a "joy" through which we learn perseverance, which will lead to our perfection. Perfection here is not of the worldly sort, concerned with looks or status, but rather, it is the perfection we achieve when we are being the person God has called us to be for his glory.

Like most gifts we are given, the fruit of joy is not meant to be kept to oneself. St. Paul's image of being poured out as a libation for others is a beautiful one. I picture a huge earthen jug, overflowing, slightly tipped over, spilling out, and covering all those we meet. Just as a drink relieves our thirst, the joy of the Holy Spirit relieves our weary souls.

An Invitation to Share

1. Make a list of the things that bring you joy. Think about the things that give you a grateful heart, the things that help you remember that God has given you so much. Compare the things on this list to the things you often encounter throughout a typical day or week. Are you spending time doing those things that bring you joy? Are you spending time with people who bring you joy?

_____

_____

_____

_____

_____

_____

_____

_____

_____

_____

_____

_____

_____

_____

2. Start a gratitude list in your Bible, planner, or journal. This is for you, not for social media. For example, one Sunday afternoon I spent a few hours sitting in my family room with my husband, our children and their spouses, and our grandson. There was no big photo opportunity and no fabulous dinner; it was just us, and it was wonderful. What will you write on your gratitude list?

_____

_____

_____

_____

_____

_____

_____

_____

_____

_____

_____

_____

_____

_____

_____

_____

_____

_____

3. Which Scripture verse about joy can you claim as your own and try to live out more fully in your life?

_____

_____

_____

_____

_____

_____

_____

_____

_____

_____

_____

_____

_____

_____

_____

_____

_____

_____

_____

_____

Closing Prayer

Lord, you show me the way to joy with your words of comfort and truth. Joy is putting Jesus first, then serving and loving others, and then ourselves. Help me to remember this every day, especially on the days when life around me seems distressing and difficult. I am called to live a life full of the fruits of the Spirit so that I can be an example of you to others who do not yet know you.

My spirit of joy is a light. Guide me in sharing it with the people in my life. Help me to be grateful and to always remember that true joy comes from you. It is through knowing your Word that I discover my true purpose, and this leads me to joy; so, create in me a thirst for your Word, Father. I give you thanks and praise and glory for all you have given me. And I give you permission to continue moving me toward the joy that comes from being your child. Amen.

2: Peace

Opening Prayer

Heavenly Father, peace is what we need in this world today—peace among nations, peoples, and families. Inside of me, there is a small seed of peace that I want to grow, and I can with your help. Teach me to find the good in others. Help me to think before I speak so that I may speak words that bring peace instead of strife.

Jesus gave us your peace before he left this earth—not as the world gives, but as only you can give. I ask the Holy Spirit to fill me with the peace that guides my heart and mind, especially in times of trouble and confusion.

Lord, that is the peace I seek—the peace that calms me when there is strife, the peace that leads me to acceptance when things do not go my way, the peace that reminds me that you are in control when chaos seems to surround me. Let, also, the peace that brings contentment to reign within me when all is well, so I may live in the present without worry for the future. I pray that your peace will be evident to others so that I can testify to all that you give me. Amen.

Peace

On My Heart

_____

_____

_____

_____

_____

_____

_____

_____

_____

_____

_____

_____

_____

_____

Cultivate Peace with the Holy Spirit

Who except God can give you peace? Has the world ever been able to satisfy the heart?

—*Saint Gerard Majella*

In the mid-1970s a song came out from Carey Landry, "Peace Is Flowing like a River." It seemed like we sang it everywhere, including Girl Scouts, school, and Mass. I even learned to play it on the guitar. One line that I loved back then and clearly remember even today is, "Peace is flowing like a river, setting all the captives free." It could be the theme of this section on this fruit of the Spirit, peace. I picture a gentle flow of water, persistently flowing over rough-edged rocks, slowly soaking into the bed of the river, meandering on its path, and eventually changing the way things look. Rough rocks become smooth and earth wears away; the water has changed the environment. The fruit of peace can change our environment as well. And, like water flowing in the river, that peace from the Holy Spirit will flow into others.

Peace sets us free. First, let's define the peace I am speaking of here. It is the peace from God that gives us strength and courage to go on in the face of difficulties. As a woman living in the twenty-first century, I don't see much peace. I see division, wars, contempt, ridicule, and strife, and this is not only out in the world but in our own homes, families, workplaces, and social circles. So many of us live at a frenetic pace, which defies the very notion of peace in our soul. To have peace in our souls, there needs to be silence in which we can soak in God's peace. How can we achieve or receive this peace if we are always busy?

Second, what is the freedom that peace gives? Our freedom comes from Christ, who redeemed us by his death on a cross. He tells us more than once in Scripture that he came so that we could have peace. In John 14:27, he says, "Peace I leave with you, my peace I give to you. Not as the world gives do I give it to you. Do not let your hearts be troubled or afraid." This peace is given to us so that we do not fear life or the world. This peace helps us to let go of our need to control everything and to trust God. His peace reminds us that we are not in control. He is.

I come from a family of six—two parents and four children, of whom I am the oldest, but not by much. My next younger brother and sister are twins born just ten months after me. Five years later, we were joined by another brother. To say there was no peace in our house is an understatement. It was loud, it was busy, and it was very full. When the twins arrived, I was quite taken with them and doted on them. Since I had learned to walk, I could fetch diapers and bottles, and be helpful. I am sure I was a great one-year-old helper to my mom! As we grew up, however, it became apparent to me that it was the twins against me. They formed a united front. Whenever there was a fight over toys, it was automatically two against one. When there was a question about who started it, again, two against one. As the oldest, I was expected to be better behaved than the younger children.

There was trouble often, sometimes serious, sometimes just messy. The serious stuff involved more than one trip to the emergency room for the twins and my little brother. The shopping cart story is legendary in the family. My mom, the twins, and I were at the grocery store. I was walking, holding onto the cart, and the twins were in the cart. When my mom turned to pick out some produce, my sister tried to climb out of the cart. As she attempted to get out she, slipped and fell onto the metal edge of the cart right on the bridge of her nose. Lots of blood and a few stitches later, she was fine, but it was frightening to see. Then there was the time my little brother broke his leg when he rolled off my sister's lap while she was sitting on the floor holding him. Then there was the fighting. We fought constantly over toys, who was taking up more room in the bedroom, whose turn it was to sit in the front seat of the car, who needed to set the table, and on and on.

I vowed that when I grew up and had a family, I would not have a tumultuous family. I would have a calm, peaceful home. My children would not fight because I would treat them fairly and respectfully. And that is just what happened—eventually.

In the beginning of establishing my own family, I still did not fully understand what peace looked like. I assumed it was all up to me, instead of realizing that I could ask for help from God. Days and months and years went by as I was constantly trying to fix the people and situations around me. When I look back, I cringe at how difficult I was to be around, all in the name of looking for peace. I had to learn that I needed to change before peace could take root in me and grow. You cannot force peace into your home and your loved ones by dictating to others how that is to happen. You cannot yell people into peacefulness.

Peace came when I accepted the marvelous reality that God is in charge. He is trustworthy, and his Word is truth. My fears and anxieties, both of the world and for my family, from the biggest problem to the smallest, could be handed to God. He would, as he promised through Jesus, give me peace.

I was working at a job that was not a good fit for me, and I had no idea what might come next for me. As God's timing is perfect, a new group for women was starting in my parish. The group's primary purpose was to praise God, pray, and learn more about living a life filled with the Holy Spirit. This was the first time I thought specifically about the gifts and fruits of the Holy Spirit. And it was amazing! I began to see the connections among the sacraments, prayer, and the fruits of the Spirit. It is like a math equation: sacraments + prayer = more fruit! This is true not only for peace but for all the fruits. My job did not change; I had to keep my position until the end of the school year, but my perspective changed. Through the sacraments and prayer, I was able to gain peace in a decidedly unpeaceful time and place. The only thing that changed was my perspective, by the help of the Holy Spirit. And the perspective is that God is bigger than all the problems and concerns. It is the belief that he cares and will provide a solution.

Why Do We Lack Peace?

One Scripture story that comes to mind when I think of peace is the calming of the storm. It is in Matthew, Mark, and Luke; I like Mark's account the best because the description of Jesus sleeping says he was "asleep on a cushion" (Mark 4:38a). This was not a head-bob little nap; he clearly intended to sleep. A storm begins to rage and yet Jesus sleeps on. The apostles are very afraid; indeed, they think they are "perishing" (Mark 4:38b), so they wake up Jesus, who then rebukes the wind and the waves, "and there was great calm" (Mark 4:39). Then he chastises the disciples, asking them, "Do you not yet have faith?" (Mark 4:40)

How many times do we run around like people stirred up and chased about by a storm? I cannot answer for you, but as for myself, it happens much more often than I like. Hurry, urgent, now, help me, feed me, play with me, answer me—all day long we are pushed and pulled. There is no peace. Why don't we go around rebuking the wind and the sea in our own life, so we can have calm? Maybe because we like the lack of peace. Maybe we like being busy or having a constant stimulus so there is never a peaceful moment within us. I know that I wore the lack of peace like a badge of honor, that is, until I decided to stop. Not every need was urgent; not every whim needed to be acted upon, nor each desire fulfilled. It takes prayer, daily prayer, and being connected to Jesus, especially in Scripture and in the Eucharist, for there to be peace in me. I want to be able to sleep in peace through the storm with Jesus, knowing God's got it. Whatever the "it" is, God will take care of it.

Maybe peace seems boring to you. I have encountered people in many situations who seem to thrive on crises and who sometimes manufacture problems where none exist. I worked in an office where we used the term "pot stirrer" for those who liked to create drama.

Creating drama is different than being a "drama queen (or king)." Creating drama puts the focus on others while a drama queen puts the focus on themselves. Either way though, the drama creates a diversion, division, or discord among others or within ourselves.

I think peace is restful. To me, peace can be equated with being sure of your purpose. When I ask for guidance and then make a decision that honors that guidance, I have peace about my decision. It may not be easy or pleasant, but peace prevails because you are doing the right thing. Not only does peace prevail but strength and courage to accomplish the task come as well.

A lack of peace can also stem from anxiety. There is internal anxiety that should be evaluated and treated and taken seriously. Anxiety can be debilitating. There is also the anxiety that seems to come from outside of us. It might be from a stimulus overload or difficult situations. Maybe you cannot sleep because you are worrying about something. When I am overloaded, my left eye twitches. If that starts, I need a break, and while a week away might be great, it cannot happen every time my eye starts twitching!

Instead, I go back to what I should be doing but am probably not doing because I am busy. I read Scripture; I pray more deliberately; I go to adoration. It may seem that the best solution is to attack the to-do list until it is all done, but taking a step back, pausing, and collecting yourself will make it easier to accomplish your goals. The added bonus is that by spending time in prayer, tasks that seemed urgent can seem more relaxed, or maybe God will tell you to delegate or disregard them.

What type of peace do you need in your life? Do you need internal or external peace? I would say, from my own experience and from talking to many people, that there must first be internal peace. Then we can begin to work on the external peace. When we give God everything that makes us anxious, frustrates us, scares us, and worries us, our burden is lightened, and we receive peace in abundance.

An Invitation to Ponder

In your own life, is there a lack of peace? Consider whether it is internal or external peace that needs attention. What is your most pressing concern that causes the lack of peace?

_____

_____

_____

_____

_____

_____

_____

_____

_____

_____

_____

_____

_____

_____

_____

_____

_____

Connecting to Scripture

PRAYER BEFORE READING SCRIPTURE

Father, fill me with the Holy Spirit to guide me as I read and reflect on your Word. I ask for the grace to allow your Word to flood my soul so that I may grow ever closer to you and your Son Jesus. Amen.

In our search for peace, God's Word will provide many examples of it. While reading through these Scriptures, here are a couple questions you can ponder: What does God speak to his people about? In what ways does Jesus restore or give people peace?

❧ Psalm 85:9 _____

_____

_____

❧ Psalm 119:165 _____

_____

_____

❧ Mark 5:24–34 _____

_____

_____

✐ John 14:15-27 _____

_____

_____

Scripture Reflection

As you read through those passages, do you see how God is reaching out to you? His desire is to set you free and give you peace. First, we must know his Word. In Scripture, we learn why God made us and that he made us for good.

In the psalms we looked at, we see how God speaks to us of peace so we do "not turn to foolishness"(Psalms 85:9). If we love God's law, we most likely also love God. And in that loving, we seek to follow his law out of love. This, in turn, keeps us on the path he has laid out for us.

In Mark's story about the woman healed of a hemorrhage, Jesus is giving her so much more than physical healing. He is giving her back her life, setting her free to live fully again as a child of God. This woman lived for twelve years without any freedom to live her life in a normal way. As a Jewish woman, she knew that she was considered to be un-clean and could not live and move about freely. She had to be vigilant in making sure to follow the cleanliness and ritual purification laws so that others would not be made unclean by contact with her. It must have been a very isolating existence. The woman was afraid to openly touch Jesus because of that uncleanliness. I also wonder, was she awed by his great power and so approached him with humility? Her thoughts show her faith and humility: "If I but touch his clothes, I shall be cured" (Mark 5:28). She had no desire to call attention to herself.

The woman with a hemorrhage needed physical healing, but also spiritual peace. I think that many of us need this peace. And we can get it. If we desire peace in ourselves, which is where it begins, we need to turn to him. Turn to him and tell him what we need. You may be wondering why I say to tell God what you need. Does he not already know? Yes, he knows, but in our asking, we show him two qualities or leanings that make our request more genuine. In our asking, we show our humility and our readiness to grow and change.

When we read John 14:27, we see how simple it is to have peace. We accept the gift Jesus has left with us. We can walk in the truth that we have peace, and we do not have to let our "hearts be troubled or afraid." Sadly, many of us complicate our spiritual lives by thinking that they are like our worldly lives. Now, I am not suggesting that our body and soul are not one; they are one hundred percent connected. But God does not operate the way that people do. In this world, we must often follow rules and jump through hoops that can seem random and unnecessary. Nothing God asks of us is random or arbitrary. It is all for our good.

It truly is a peace that surpasses all understanding, as St. Paul tells us in Philippians 4:6-7, "Have no anxiety at all, but in everything, by prayer and petition, with thanksgiving, make your requests known to God. Then the peace of God that surpasses all understanding will guard your hearts and minds in Christ Jesus."

An Invitation to Share

1. What robs you of the peace Jesus has given us through the Holy Spirit? Is it your schedule, the demands of others, your attempts to control every situation? In prayer, ask the Holy Spirit to show you what robs you of your peace, and then make some notes about ways you might remedy the situations.

---

2. How can you give yourself the gift of time to be still, even if just for a minute each day, to ask for the peace of the Spirit?

_____

_____

_____

_____

_____

_____

_____

_____

_____

_____

_____

_____

_____

_____

_____

_____

_____

_____

_____

_____

_____

_____

3. What does peace look like in your life? Remember, each of us has a different level of tolerance and ability in terms of our responsibilities. Are there things you need to remove from your life? And, dare I ask, is there something you need to add?

_____

_____

_____

_____

_____

_____

_____

_____

_____

_____

_____

_____

_____

_____

_____

_____

_____

_____

_____

_____

_____

Closing Prayer

Lord, you have shown me that you long for me to have peace even more than I want it myself. Guide me to those things which help me have peace, and root out of me whatever keeps me from peace. I know that I can turn to you, your Word, and your sacraments in times of need. I thank you for those gifts and for the desire to grow closer to you through them. Trade my sorrow for joy, and my unrest for peace. Help me to live in peace so that others may come to know you through me. I ask this all in the name of Jesus and the Holy Spirit.

Amen.

Peace

3: Patience

Opening Prayer

Lord, you have given me all that I have and need. Sometimes I take it for granted in wanting more, in demanding instead of asking, and in expecting instead of being grateful. Yet you are infinitely patient with me, leading me to be still and wait—for you.

Help me to bear the imperfections of others, because I know that I am not perfect and that I need your mercy and forgiveness. As Teresa of Avila said, "Let nothing disturb you, let nothing frighten you, all things are passing away: God never changes. Patience obtains all things, whoever has God lacks nothing; God alone suffices."[3]

Patience is needed so I can be close to you, remembering as St. Teresa said that patience will get you everything you need, most especially God, and if I have God, I will lack not one thing because God is all. Open my soul to know that I have you and that is all I need. Help me, Lord, to be as patient with others as you are with me. Teach me to be more like you in all I do. Amen.

Patience

On My Heart

_____

_____

_____

_____

_____

_____

_____

_____

_____

_____

_____

_____

Cultivate Patience with the Holy Spirit

This chapter focuses on the fruit of the Spirit of patience. Just think-ing about patience may cause us to cringe as we remember last night's bedtime routine, which turned into a wrestling match among the children, or an argument that erupted with a coworker. Compared to joy, which sounds so light, patience certainly sounds like hard work may be involved. Fear not, we can gain patience. Why do I say that? Because I have learned patience. By the grace of God, this always-in-a-rush, do-it-my-way, waiting-is-not-for-me woman has changed. I am not perfect, but I do not struggle with it in the same way as I did in the past. I have come to appreciate waiting. What matters is that we continue to pray and grow, remembering that progress is important and that God will supply us with what we lack when we need it.

Patience may be one of the fruits of the Spirit that we avoid thinking about. Our society is not known for having patience. We like instant gratification—the quick method, overnight shipping, fast relief, and no waiting. At least, when we are on the receiving end that is what we want. Flip it around and we get annoyed when others have those expectations of us. Patience has become synonymous with waiting. Be it at the doctor's office, in the supermarket check-out line, or at dinner, waiting seems like a waste of time. But waiting is unavoidable. Life takes time. Life is not without trials and struggles. How we react to those trials and struggles is often a measure of our patience. Some days the struggle is getting children dressed for school, while on others it is how to pay the mortgage after your husband has lost his job. Our reaction to what happens in our life is our choice. We can lash out, become irritated, or find fault with others when we lack patience. And so, cultivating patience is a worthwhile endeavor.

Notice that I do not say to pray for patience. Why? I think we need to take responsibility for our actions, and sometimes, if we pray for something, we forget that we, also, need to do something to work toward the goal. We should pray and ask for help in learning to be patient, but saying, "Father, please give me patience" might sound like we think it is going to arrive—poof—like an Amazon Prime delivery. It is not; we gain patience by practicing patience with the help of our Father.

"Please be patient" is a request we might hear in a busy office or on the phone waiting for customer service. What are we being asked in these situations? To not get frustrated with waiting and to trust that our turn will come as soon as possible and that our needs will be met at that time. What do we do while we are waiting shows whether we have patience or not. Do you read a book or magazine or check email? Or do you make quiet, or maybe not-so-quiet, comments to others around you about how busy you are and how slow the staff is in taking care of people? How we behave when we have to wait is a mark of our level of patience.

Waiting on God

The book of Exodus has many examples of different types of patience. There is the patience of Moses' mother as she hides Moses, trusting that God would take care of him. We see the patience of God when Moses asks him more than once if he (God) is sure that he (Moses) is the right man for the job of getting the Israelites out of Egypt. There is, also, the patience of Moses as he deals, first, with Pharaoh, and then with his own people on the journey through the desert.

In Exodus 24 Moses and God seal the covenant made between God and the Israelites. Moses leaves Aaron and the elders in charge of the people while he goes to meet with God and receive the stone tablets. He is on the mountain for forty days and nights. Meanwhile, back at the bottom of the mountain, the people there, who have no idea how important the meeting between God and Moses is, are getting restless and bored.

Imagine the scene: your leader, who has slain the Egyptians, who asked God to give you food and water, who led you out of slavery, is with God, and you are waiting. The Israelites are getting agitated. Instead of waiting with patience and trust, they decide to go to Aaron. Chapter 32 of Exodus finds Aaron being convinced by the people to make a molten calf out of the golden earrings everyone is wearing. Aaron melts the gold and makes a calf. They set up an altar to the calf and make sacrifices to it, turning it into a big party. The Israelites had very quickly turned away from the covenant with God because of a total lack of patience. Have we ever taken matters into our own hands to "make things happen" instead of waiting?

In this example, the people are waiting on God, and God does not take it lightly when we choose to not wait for him. He says, "I have seen this people, how stiff-necked they are" (Exodus 32:9). That stings, does it not? God is not mincing words here, and it reminds me to not be so stubborn. I look at stubbornness as a trait that accompanies a lack of patience. Think about how many times we do not want to wait or ask for help or look at another solution. We want to do it our way, now! We know best, so we rush into a decision, and then we live with the consequences.

One of my favorite stories in the Old Testament that reminds me of how God works is of the prophet Elijah. Like so many of the prophets, he was not welcomed with open arms when he told the people to stop worshipping idols and turn back to God. Eventually, he swayed the people, but only after a great show of force by God, and then Elijah, himself, killed the false prophets. This did not win him favor with the King's wife, Jezebel, who swore to kill him. So, he fled to "the mountain of God, Horeb" (1 Kings 19:8). He was invited to meet God and so Elijah stood on the mountain, waiting through wind, an earthquake, and fire before he finally heard God in a light sound.

Being Patient with Others and Ourselves

We yell at our husbands, do not take a minute to consider our co-workers' ideas, nag our children to hurry, or scream at the slow drivers. Our lives seem to fly by at an uncontrolled pace, moving from one task to another, with no time to rest in between, no way to exercise patience, because it is all about now and all about me. We have those days, do we not, when this is how we live, giving no one, least of all ourselves, a minute's peace?

And yet, when we think about all that God has done for us and the patience he shows us, we know that living this way is not what he wants. How can we have patience with others? I think one way may be to lower our expectations. Yes, I suggested lowering our expectations for two reasons. It was said to me many, many years ago by my confessor, and it helps. It really does.

If we are expecting others to do things the way we would, we are bound to be disappointed. It helps to remember that there is usually more than one way to complete a task. Just because it is not your way does not mean that it is the wrong way. Especially when we are teaching others how to do certain things, trying and demonstrating progress on their part is important, and we need to recognize that.

Learning takes time, and if your tendency is to step in so that tasks are done quickly, than others lose a learning opportunity. If your three-year-old wants to dress herself, try to leave enough time before you need to leave the house so she can do it. And while you can finish putting together the work e-newsletter quickly because you've been doing it for so long, not handing it over to the new person because you are faster is not right. St. Paul reminds the Thessalonians and us when he says, "We urge you, brothers, admonish the idle, cheer the faint-hearted, support the weak, be patient with all" (1 Thessalonians 5:14).

When I take the time to lower my expectations I see the person with whom I am losing patience in a different light. I focus on the effort being made and the fact that they are doing their best, and doing something (usually) is better than nothing. Sometimes that person I am losing patience with is me. I am hard on myself, and it has taken years to learn that good enough is good enough.

I love to sew. I have been making clothes for myself and others since I was in high school. Recently I have taken up quilting, but I am not very good at it. I am not sure if it is the cutting or sewing together part, but things do not square up correctly. I make the quilts anyway, however, for the people I love. I doubt I will ever receive the same compliments on my quilts as I do on my clothes, but it is okay. I'm lowering my expectations rather than losing patience and quitting. And I hope, with practice, I will improve.

Then, of course, there is this important question: do you have patience with yourself? Have you ever been multitasking, convinced that you can do all five things on your desk simultaneously, but when you need to print something, it just will not print? That is me on a regular basis. And usually the document will not print because I think that I am hitting the print button, but I am not. Total user error caused by my belief that I can do everything at once!

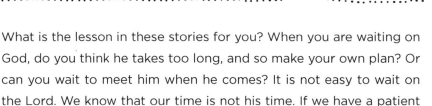

An Invitation to Ponder

What is the lesson in these stories for you? When you are waiting on God, do you think he takes too long, and so make your own plan? Or can you wait to meet him when he comes? It is not easy to wait on the Lord. We know that our time is not his time. If we have a patient disposition, we often learn something necessary and important in a time of waiting.

_____

_____

_____

_____

_____

_____

_____

_____

_____

_____

_____

_____

_____

_____

_____

_____

_____

Connecting to Scripture

PRAYER BEFORE READING SCRIPTURE

Father, fill me with the Holy Spirit to guide me as I read and reflect on your Word. I ask for the grace to allow your word to flood my soul that I may grow ever closer to you and your Son Jesus. Amen.

❧ Proverbs 15:18 and 16:32_____

_____

_____

🖋 Ecclesiastes 3:18 _____

_____

_____

🖋 Romans 2:4-8 _____

_____

_____

🖋 James 5:7-11 _____

_____

_____

🖋 2 Peter 3:9 _____

_____

_____

Scripture Reflection

Once we learn how God is patient with us and where we need to grow in patience, we can look at how we are supposed to treat others. Our patience, or lack thereof, influences those around us. It is easy to lose patience with people when they do not meet our expectations. This includes everyone from the toddler who will not keep his shoes on, to our friend who is often late to meet us, to family members who stray from the faith. If you, like me, do not find patience quick or easy to come by, pausing and praying is very helpful.

Like all of us, I am working on patience. What makes me impatient? I will give you a short list since I am asking you to do the same.

- *others taking forever to leave the house*

- *changing your mind for no good reason after a decision is made, especially if I have started to execute that decision*

- *always waiting for someone else to do it*

- *channel surfing*

- *traffic, especially when paired with construction*

The verses from Proverbs remind us that a person who has patience can settle disputes, can calm other people, and can be "better than warriors" (Proverbs 16:32a). Clearly, it is considered an important virtue in the Old Testament as well as in the New Testament. Do we strive for patience or allow ourselves to have an ill temper which causes problems?

Something Will Change

The world is constantly changing and moving from one time to another, as we are reminded in Ecclesiastes 3:1–8. There are many times in our own lives when times or seasons of our lives merge together, when times to weep and mourn seem to come with laughing and dancing. I think that is life in all its fullness. These verses also point to the need for patience. In some ways, they are telling us "wait, something will change," and it does. The tearing down turns to building up, silence to speaking, and scattering to gathering. So, hold on, because whatever season you are in, it will change. While we are in the season, we need to do our best to practice patience.

The more we know about God, the more we love him and, in turn, want to serve and honor him. God desires us to be fully free to love, honor, and serve him. He is very patient with us, so we will be led to repentance and overcome our stubbornness and unforgiveness, as St. Paul says in Romans 2:4-8.

The Patience of a Prophet

When St. James speaks of patience, he recommends we take the example of the prophets (James 5:10). I spoke of Moses at the beginning of this chapter; he is an excellent example of patience, though the people he led often had none. Other prophets that come to mind are: Jonah, once he stopped fighting with God about going to Nineveh; and Isaiah, who served God for many years, exhorting the people to turn back to him. They were faithful to God, to their calling, and to the people they served. They showed great patience among many trials. We can see how sometimes what appears to be waiting for no reason is actually God waiting until we or others have come to repentance, as Peter reminds us in 2 Peter 3:9. That time of waiting, frustrating as it may be, gives us an opportunity to turn away from sin or to discern the best course of action. It is a gift God gives us, not a punishment.

It is my hope that one day we will all be blessed in our perseverance of cultivating patience.

An Invitation to Share

1. Make a list of things, situations, and people that make you impatient. Pick three of them and determine the reason they cause you impatience. Pray about each one and make a plan to help you be more patient in each set of circumstances.

_____

_____

_____

_____

_____

_____

_____

_____

_____

_____

_____

_____

_____

_____

_____

_____

_____

_____

_____

_____

_____

_____

_____

_____

_____

_____

_____

_____

_____

_____

2. Is it more of a struggle for you to have patience with God or with life circumstances and people? Why?

_____

_____

_____

_____

_____

_____

_____

_____

_____

_____

_____

_____

_____

_____

_____

3. Do you believe that having more patience is important? If so, how do you think it will help you on your faith journey?

_____

_____

_____

_____

_____

_____

_____

_____

_____

_____

_____

_____

_____

_____

Closing Prayer

Thank you, Father, for reminding me of your patience with me. You are constant and forgiving, waiting for me to draw close to you. You wait, watching me learn to have patience. There is no better example of patience than you; from when you choose the Israelites to be your people to sending your Son Jesus to save us to now, you have shown infinite patience. I am grateful for that. Help me, Father, to grow in my patience, so that I am a better example to others. My hope is to be able to wait on you and then follow your will with love and patience. Life may not always go as planned, but if I wait with a patient attitude, I will show the Spirit that is within me and draw others to your Son. I know following you does not mean my life will be easy or free of trials. Please allow the Holy Spirit to fill me with an abundance of patience for those trials of life. I believe that with you at my side, I will learn patience. As always, I thank you for all that you have given me.

Amen.

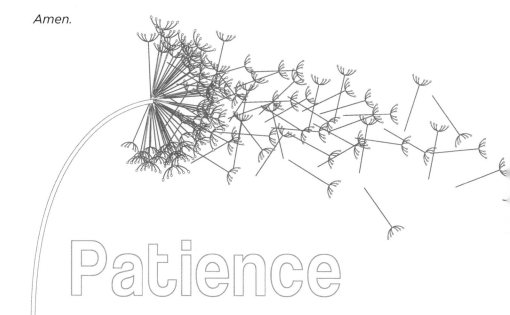

4: Faithfulness

INVITE THE HOLY SPIRIT

Opening Prayer

You, O God, are the ultimate example of faithfulness.

In all of Scripture, from Adam and Eve to the Israelites to sending your Son Jesus to save me, you have always been faithful to me, your daughter. I have not always been faithful to you, and for that, I ask for your forgiveness and mercy. Help me, Father, to learn how to be faithful to you, to your will for me, and to the people you have given me to care for in my life. Help me learn to live out faithfulness every day, remembering that those who are faithful in small matters learn to be faithful in all matters.

May the Holy Spirit fill me with the desire to be a person who can be trusted to act according to the Commandments and the Beatitudes. Turning to you, my most faithful Father, I ask you to be with me, today and always.

Amen.

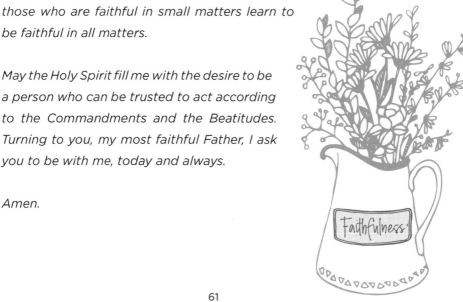

Faithfulness

On My Heart

_____

_____

_____

_____

_____

_____

_____

_____

_____

_____

_____

_____

_____

_____

_____

_____

Cultivate Faithfulness with the Holy Spirit

God has not called me to be successful, he has called me to be faithful.

—St. Teresa of Calcutta

There are two ways to look at faithfulness in Scripture. One is how God is faithful, and the other is how we are faithful. We will look at both in turn because both are important and necessary. We may not have ever thought about how faithful God is to us, but in Scripture, there is a long history of it. It begins back with the story of creation and has not ended since that time. All around us are examples of God's faithfulness to us, yet often our eyes are not opened enough to see them. Why is that? It could be because faithfulness is not something you see much in our society. We live in a time that says very little is worth sticking to unless it suits my purpose and plan. Abortion and divorce are the most obvious examples of a lack of faithfulness. Choices are made, and then we are surprised at the consequences or results of those choices.

Faithfulness often requires putting aside our own needs and desires for a time for the good of another. It may be a sacrifice to do this, but it is a worthwhile one.

God's Faithfulness

Let us turn first to the fact that God is faithful and what that means for us in our daily lives. Have you ever thought of how God is faithful to us? The more you read his Word, the more you see that faithfulness in terms of what he has done for his people as an entity. God called Abraham into a covenant with him, promising descendants and land. God was faithful to that promise even though Abraham often lied and failed to trust God. Eventually, Abraham came to know God and to trust him fully. The test Abraham faced—that of God asking him to sacrifice his only son Isaac—is an example of how much Abraham trusted God. Abraham never sacrificed Isaac, but he was willing to do what God had asked. His response to God's faithfulness was to be faithful to God.

Another example we may be familiar with is the story of how God took his people out of Egypt and brought them to the promised land. No matter how much they complained, no matter how much they disobeyed, and no matter how much they questioned God, he never deserted them. He was a visible sign in their midst in the pillar of fire, in the manna, in the quail, in the water, and in the Ten Commandments; yet they still did not remain faithful to him. It was his faithfulness, not theirs, that finally brought them to the promised land after wandering in the desert for forty years.

The entire Old Testament is one example after another of God's faithfulness. When the people strayed, he sent prophets, judges, and kings to call them back to him. Over and over, God remembered his side of the covenants and promises he made and wanted to help his people to remain faithful to him. Some did remain faithful, while others did not.

We know how the story continues; God the Father sends his Son Jesus to save us, and after Jesus's resurrection, we are gifted with the Holy Spirit. The first words we encounter in Matthew's Gospel tell the genealogy of Jesus. It begins with Abraham and continues all the way to Joseph, naming the fathers who became the fathers. It includes three mothers, Tamar, Ruth, and Mary. This genealogy, just as others in the Bible, reminds us of God's faithfulness to his people.

In John's Gospel, there is a striking example of faithfulness in the raising of Lazarus from the dead. This is a very personal story about Jesus and his friends, Mary, Martha, and Lazarus. These are not nameless followers or people seeking Jesus for their own needs. They are his friends, who offer to Jesus companionship, hospitality, and a place to rest away from crowds and demands.

Except for that one time, when Lazarus is sick. Worried for their brother, who is gravely ill, Mary and Martha send for Jesus. In an unexpected move, Jesus waits before going to Bethany, saying, "This illness is not to end in death, but is for the glory of God, that the Son of God may be glorified through it" (John 11:4). Lazarus dies while Jesus is on his way, and Martha runs out to meet him, telling Jesus that if he had been there, her brother would not have died. Jesus goes to Lazarus's tomb; he weeps. Then Jesus commands the stone to be rolled away, saying to his Father, "I know that you always hear me" (John 11:42a), and commands Lazarus to come out of the tomb. We see Jesus being faithful to his friends, and we hear Jesus reminding us that the Father is always faithful in listening to us.

We have ample evidence of God's faithfulness, and yet, how often in our own lives do we question whether he is paying attention? After all of those examples of God saving everyone, is he really concerned about us? Do we know that our Father hears us? Do we believe that he knows our needs and will provide for them?

At one point in my life, I worked as a youth minister. I had always wanted to work in a parish so it was a dream come true. The religious education director was a friend and a woman I looked up to. She was a great mentor, and we worked very well together. Our parish took on a new life, and we knew that God was with us in our efforts. All of our work and efforts seemed pointless, though, after a new pastor came and many changes were made. I was forced to leave my job and, eventually, I left the parish. It was too painful to be there. I questioned God for weeks and months. Many of us were hurt, angry, and confused. By grace, I did not lose my faith. Why? Because at every turn, somehow, my life was still intact. I was in shock and not sure how I could carry on with any semblance of normalcy for my children. But the summer break schedule was on my side, which meant our son was off to camp and our daughter to my parents' house for two weeks, giving me the time and space to grieve. My husband and I were in the process of buying a home when I lost my job. We had understood that obtaining the mortgage would be dependent on both our salaries, yet everything went through.

There was no doubt in my mind, months later, that it was God's hand on me, his faithfulness that got me through one of the worst times of my life. If you look back, you will find your own story of God's faithfulness in your life.

The best news, though, is that it happens over and over again.

Our Faithfulness

The most important relationship to remain faithful to is between God and yourself. The primacy of that relationship cannot be overstated. As if you had a camera in your hand, pull back from your life and look around you, pulling back further and further, seeing the world. There is war, destruction, devastation, greed, fighting for control, abuse of power, hatred, and so much more. There is a lack of decency in how people treat each other. When I look, I often see that God is missing in their lives. If you follow God and follow him with humility, then, when you encounter others, you spread the Good News and share what you have been given. How we live out our life on a day-to-day basis is important.

Look at the widow of Zarephath in 1 Kings 17. At God's command, the prophet Elijah goes to her for bread and water. She tells Elijah that she has just enough to make a small cake for herself and her son, and then they will die because they have no more food. Elijah tells her that God will make sure that the flour and oil jars will not go empty if she helps Elijah. She is faithful and has trust in God; in turn, God is faithful to her. Though there is a drought, she always has enough flour and oil. Later in the chapter, the widow's son gets sick, and the widow comes to Elijah, blaming him for her son's sickness (1 Kings 17: 14–24). Elijah calls out to God, asking him why the son is sick. He prays to God, stretching himself over the dying boy three times. God answers his prayer, and the woman says to Elijah, "Now indeed I know that you are a man of God, and it is truly the word of the Lord that you speak" (1 Kings 17:24).

The hard part about faithfulness is that we may sometimes be asked to stay in a situation that is very difficult. For many years, I have been friends with a woman who is not physically healthy. She has a host of autoimmune diseases, has had heart attacks, a stroke, and had to have her small and large intestines removed. She is married and has a daughter. Her husband has stood by her, going from being married to a woman who worked, sang in church, painted, sewed, cooked, was a catechist, and danced, to a woman who is almost bedridden. As her illnesses have progressed, she has lost many friends. She has lost the ability to focus enough to read, to sing, to walk unassisted, to drive. To the world, she has lost so much, yet looked upon with eyes of faith, she still has so much.

She has tremendous faith and a dedication to the Blessed Mother. Her husband never wavers from her side. One day, another friend and I visited her in the hospital while she was intubated and sedated. Her husband stood by her head and gently brushed her hair off her face and put it into a ponytail. In the loving way he looked at her, it appeared as though he was trying to will her to good health. The scene was so touching, it almost made me cry. He is faithful to her.

It takes strength to be faithful. And that strength comes from God.

An Invitation to Ponder

When has your faithfulness been tested? It may have been a test of faith in God or in a relationship. Were you ever led to a place you did not think you could survive, and yet you did? Did you see God's hand on you?

_____

_____

_____

_____

_____

_____

_____

_____

_____

_____

_____

_____

_____

_____

_____

_____

_____

_____

_____

_____

_____

_____

_____

Connecting to Scripture

PRAYER BEFORE READING SCRIPTURE

Father, fill me with the Holy Spirit to guide me as I read and reflect on your Word. I ask for the grace to allow your Word to flood my soul that I may grow ever closer to you and your Son Jesus. Amen.

✍ Psalm 89:2-3; 89:9 _____

_____

_____

✍ Psalm 89:34 _____

_____

_____

✍ Wisdom 3:1-9 _____

_____

_____

✍ Sirach 1:27 _____

_____

_____

⁊ Hebrews 3:1–6 _____

_____

_____

Scripture Reflection

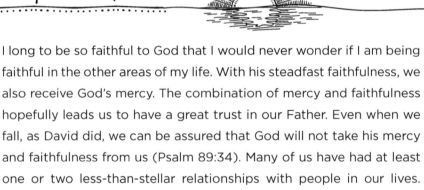

I long to be so faithful to God that I would never wonder if I am being faithful in the other areas of my life. With his steadfast faithfulness, we also receive God's mercy. The combination of mercy and faithfulness hopefully leads us to have a great trust in our Father. Even when we fall, as David did, we can be assured that God will not take his mercy and faithfulness from us (Psalm 89:34). Many of us have had at least one or two less-than-stellar relationships with people in our lives. Sometimes, it is our parents or another family member. Maybe friends or coworkers have let us down. It may be a marriage that has been torn apart by a lack of faithfulness. In looking at God's Word, we learn that his faithfulness surpasses all others. His example is there for us as we live our life. Our faithfulness will be rewarded when we pass from this life into the next, and we shall live with God in love (Wisdom 3:9).

Are we faithful to what God has asked of us, no matter how big or small? As it says in Luke 16:10, "The person who is trustworthy in very small matters is also trustworthy in great ones; and the person who is dishonest in very small matters is also dishonest in great ones." I used that verse many times when my children were growing up to teach them not to lie or break promises, and to do what was asked of them. I think learning faithfulness and trustworthiness starts at a young age.

God is there for us at every turn, no matter how hard. He will never leave us or forsake us. In fact, it is God's delight when we are faithful and have humility (Sirach 1:27). Now, I know God loves me no matter what, but the idea that I can delight God? Has that ever occurred to you? We can delight him! I smile when I think about God being delighted with us, his children.

Jesus' entire life is one of faithfulness. Every page of the Gospels points to faithfulness and trust in his Father. In the most poignant scene, in the garden of Gethsemane, Jesus is praying, pleading, sweating blood as he says, "Take this cup away from me, but not what I will but what you will" (Mark 14:36), which leads him to the ultimate sign of faithfulness, the cross. That is where we see how faithful the Father and the Son are, to each other and to us. Crosses are not easy, are they? Jesus suffered a very real and painful death on his cross. What cross do you carry in the name of faithfulness to God?

My husband is a deacon, and before he started on the path to ordination, I had to give written permission. I wasn't sure about this at all. From the outside, being the family of a deacon looks great, but it comes with a price, as does all ministry. I realized that out of faithfulness to God and my marriage vows, I had to say yes. As with many crosses, some days it is light while on others I just want to put it down.

In Hebrews, Paul reminds us that as great as Moses was, he was still God's servant. Jesus is God's Son and so he can rule over God's house with the same authority as the Father. Since God has placed Jesus over his house, and Jesus is faithful to his Father, we, too, can be assured of God's faithfulness to us. As the Father's Son, Jesus has full authority over us. And as the Father is faithful and deserves our faithfulness in return, so does the Son.

An Invitation to Share

1. Make a list of the things in your life that require you to be faithful if you want a positive outcome. I'll start:

✐ prayer

✐ exercise

✐ paying attention to my husband

2. Do you believe that God is paying attention to your life? What is he asking you to trust him with now? Where is he asking you to be faithful? In prayer, turn that area, that concern, over to him, relying on his faithfulness.

_____

_____

_____

_____

_____

_____

_____

_____

_____

_____

_____

_____

_____

_____

_____

_____

_____

_____

_____

_____

3. What is your favorite story of faithfulness from the Gospels? Write a short synopsis of it here. If you know what book and chapter and verse, note it; if not, type key words into a search engine, look at the possibilities, and look them up in your Bible until you find your favorite story.

_____

_____

_____

_____

_____

_____

_____

_____

_____

_____

_____

_____

_____

_____

_____

_____

_____

_____

_____

_____

Closing Prayer

God, you have given me everything, and I praise you and glorify you for all you have done in my life, and for what you continue to do. Faithfulness, Father, is what you have shown through the ages. In every time, no matter how far your people strayed, you called them back to you, reminding them that they are yours and you are theirs. Out of love, you have given me so much, just as you gave to all those before me. Thank you for your faithfulness when I have not given you mine. Thank you for the mercy you show me when I lose heart or lack trust. I desire faithfulness. I ask, with humility and trust, for the fruit of faithfulness to grow in me. Lead me, Father, to faithfulness in what the Church teaches. If I do not understand, teach me. Lead me, Jesus, to be as faithful to your Father as you were in the Garden, accepting death on a cross for me. Holy Spirit, help me improve my faithfulness in those areas that need work. Root out mistrust. Fill me with your faithfulness. I ask all of this through the power of the Holy Spirit.

Amen.

Faithfulness

5: Kindness and Goodness

Opening Prayer

Father, the Holy Spirit's fruits of kindness and goodness seem to have left the world presently. I know this is not what you want. Help me, Lord, to begin to sow the seeds of kindness and goodness in my daily life. Teach me to return rudeness with kindness. Help me to speak your words of humility rather than my words of wanting to be right.

My desire is to be a good example of one who knows, loves, and follows your commandments. I believe that sharing kindness and goodness will make me more like the person you are calling me to be. I hope, too, that it leads others to you, reminding them that the Holy Spirit is for all who ask.

As I study your words, Lord, I know that I want them to become a part of me, my soul, my daily life. Take from me whatever stands in the way of this—my quick tongue, my sarcasm, my lack of caring—and replace it with the belief that I can be kind and good. Guide me to seek out opportunities to share these fruits with others. I trust, Father, that in the asking and in my studying, you will give me what you know I need.

Send your Spirit to be with me and to fill me, leading me always closer to you. Amen.

On My Heart

_____

_____

_____

_____

_____

_____

_____

_____

_____

_____

_____

_____

_____

Cultivate Kindness and Goodness with the Holy Spirit

What synonyms come to mind when you think about the words "kindness" and "goodness"? These are my words: nice, sweet, holy, thoughtful, helpful, and gracious. I picture an older lady with a southern accent getting some sweet tea for me while saying, "bless your heart" on a hot summer day. Never mind that I do not like sweet tea or know anyone like this!

I do know many people who exhibit kindness and goodness as part of who they are every day. I am thinking of a friend who sends cards and letters, by mail, to her family and friends all around the country or just next door. She is a gardener and shares little bouquets for no reason at all except to share the beauty of flowers and bring a smile to your face. Is her neighbor unable to get to the grocery store or in need of a meal? She helps them. I have been blessed to have this friend in my life for many years now. Many of us say, "When I grow up, I want to be like her!"

Well, we can be like her now, by cultivating the fruits of kindness and goodness. I wonder if these two fruits have fallen out of favor? Maybe they are equated with being taken advantage of, or maybe we want to be kind and good only to those who deserve it or will repay us? I know that sometimes people mistake goodness and kindness for a lack of backbone, being naive, or easily swayed. I have seen it many times. My friend and I worked together, and there were many times when other people tried to get their own way, thinking it would go unnoticed or unchallenged. Kind and good do not mean clueless! So why, then, should we even try to be kind and good?

For one thing, it is our call as Christians. In Matthew's Gospel, 5:38–42, Jesus tells us:

- *that we are not to retaliate when slapped,*

- *to give your cloak and your tunic,*

- *to go the extra mile for someone, and*

- *to always give to those in need.*

This seems extreme and countercultural, and maybe even against common sense. Jesus speaks these words for a reason. He wants to impress upon us that following him is countercultural, and it makes sense only when we look at his words in light of what we have been given by God.

In the Old Testament, kindness and goodness are attributed God and given by God to others. They remind God's people that he is with them, and the people are encouraged to share these gifts with others. God treats us with kindness and goodness, and so we, in turn, should treat others in the same way. It is rare that God gives us something to keep just for ourselves. Most gifts are given and meant to be shared with others.

Micah 6:8 could be looked at as a brief summary of how God wants us to behave: "You have been told, O mortal, what is good, and what the LORD requires of you: Only to do justice and to love goodness, and to walk humbly with your God." God has given us the rules or guidelines for our life; he has also given us free will. And that is often where the problem lies. Free will can cause us to think too much about ourselves and to forget to think about others. It can also lead us to thinking that other people should be good and kind to us before we will do the same. God, however, doesn't operate on a quid-pro-quo system.

I often keep in my head a little running list of reasons it is so difficult to be kind and good. The list all revolves around me, of course, and it goes like this:

- *I'm tired.*

- *I'm hungry.*

- *I know better.*

- *I'm right.*

↬ *People are not nice.*

↬ *I want it done my way.*

↬ *You are annoying me.*

↬ *Why should I care about you if you don't care about me?*

↬ *I really need some coffee.*

↬ *It's not fair.*

↬ *When will they be nice to me?*

↬ *Why do I always have to be the one?*

I'm trusting you to not judge me here. I can justify, based on my list, why I don't need to even try to be good or kind. Here is a true and not nice story about me not living out the gifts of kindness or goodness. My car was rear ended and was repaired while I was traveling. A few days after I got back, I turned on the radio, and the indicator light started flashing, asking me to put the code in for the radio. I looked in the glove compartment for the manual with the code, but I couldn't find the manual there. I couldn't find it anywhere, so I called the body shop where my car had been for a month. They didn't have it. I didn't believe the technician on the phone, so I started yelling, just scream-ing, and insisting they had to have the manual. I was awful. My de-fense is that my husband was in the hospital and I was overwhelmed, so I lashed out at the body shop tech. Did I ever find the manual you wonder? Why, yes, I did; it was in the house.

In the end, the number one reason we all struggle with kindness and goodness is a lack of prayer. While there is a truth in that when we have our own cares, worries, or needs which are not being taken care of it is difficult to be kind and good, our life circumstances are not an excuse to behave however we choose. In those times and situations, it is good to ask for help and take a break if possible.

Many years ago, my friend died of ovarian cancer. The day after she died I went to work, which, in hindsight, was a mistake. I spent the day doing mindless tasks and putting together final arrangements for the funeral and reception, since I worked at the parish where it was to be held. At some point the phone was ringing and ringing, so I answered it.

A woman began telling me about the death of her boyfriend, how no one would help her, and that she was having a fight with the family, and then she started in on the Church and the rules for funerals. She did not pause at all, and her volume kept escalating until she exclaimed, "You have no idea what it's like to lose someone you love!"

Typically, I am the person who can help get to the heart of the problem, address concerns, explain the rules, and arrive at a solution. This was not a typical situation. I had two choices, okay, maybe three, but hanging up on her did not seem to be an appropriate response to the situation.

I could tell her what I was going through, or I could find the parish secretary to help her. As gently as possible, I told her that I was sorry for her loss and that I would find the right person for her to speak with. After I had worked very hard to stay calm to listen and point her to the right person, she hung up. Later in the week I checked with the secretary and found that she never had called back.

I was able to exhibit some level of kindness and goodness because I did know what it was like to lose someone I loved. I was also able to do it because the entire time my friend was dying, I was steeped in prayer. And when I was not praying, I was being prayed for by others.

We need to have a "store of goodness" as it says in Matthew 12:35: "A good person brings forth good out of a store of goodness, but an evil person brings forth evil out of a store of evil."

An Invitation to Ponder

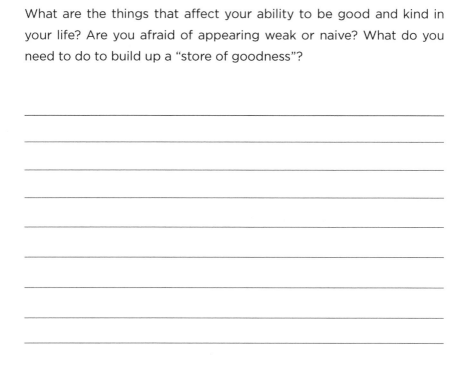

What are the things that affect your ability to be good and kind in your life? Are you afraid of appearing weak or naive? What do you need to do to build up a "store of goodness"?

_____

_____

_____

_____

_____

_____

_____

_____

_____

_____

_____

Connecting to Scripture

PRAYER BEFORE READING SCRIPTURE

Father, fill me with the Holy Spirit to guide me as I read and reflect on your Word. I ask for the grace to allow your Word to flood my soul so that I may grow ever closer to you and your Son Jesus. Amen.

❧ Psalm 23:6 _____

_____

_____

❧ Psalm 25:7-8 _____

_____

_____

❧ Psalm 69:14 _____

_____

_____

❧ Proverbs 21:21 _____

_____

_____

⁊ Sirach 3:14-16 and 3:31 _____

_____

_____

⁊ Romans 2:4 _____

_____

_____

⁊ Ephesians 5:8-9 _____

_____

_____

Scripture Reflection

God wants us to be with him, to know him, and to be like him. And so, he covers us with his goodness and kindness, willingly sharing it with us for our good and for the good of the world. We cannot say, "Thanks," and move on; our call is to act as it says in James 1:22, "Be doers of the word and not hearers only, deluding yourselves."

In the verses from Psalms and Proverbs, we see God's goodness and kindness being called upon again and again. Each time, he responds by extending mercy, forgiveness, and support. Our sins are forgotten because of his mercy and goodness (Psalm 25:7–8). Think about that for a minute: God not only forgives us, but he forgets our sins! Totally different from human thought, which is often, "I'll forgive, but I won't forget." Of course, we do not want to forget; we do not want to look foolish if we are wronged over and over. We want to protect ourselves, but clearly that is not God's way. I think about God's mercy and goodness frequently. First, I am in awe of how all-encompassing it is—nothing is too big or too small for him to forgive if we are contrite. Second, when I want to hold back kindness and goodness from someone who has hurt me, I go to God. And each time I go to him, he gently reminds me of what he has given me and tells me I need to share it with others.

Do you ever wonder if God hears, listens, or responds to your prayers? I do, and probably more often than I should. We have a history, he and I, and when I look at my life, I know he has been listening. But you don't need to take my word for it; it is in Psalm 69:14 that we are reminded that God answers us in his "abundant kindness." He does not respond with just the usual sort of kindness we expect from others, but, rather, God is abundant in his giving to us. Although it's not easy to emulate this kindness, we can try. It can be as simple as folding the laundry someone left in the dryer or making someone who has had a rough week their favorite dinner without making a big deal about it. I know someone who will go out of her way to do something for someone else and then will talk about it over and over hoping for accolades.

Sirach 3:14–16 and 3:31 remind us that our kindness to others will be given back to us in our own time of need or trouble. That's not the only reason to be kind, though. There are other rewards or benefits. We will find life, honor, and support in our struggles from others who are like us. Our kindness to our parents is looked upon as an offering for sin. How often do we take our parents for granted, even as adults? It may be difficult to honor parents who were abusive or did not take care of us properly. However, sometimes we hold onto our hurts from childhood and allow that to prevent us from have a good relationship with our parents now. This is where remembering that our parents did the best they could at that time can help us.

St. Paul reminds us in Romans 2:2–4 that we should hold God's kindness in high esteem. Why? By God's kindness, we will be led to repentance. To live a life filled with the Spirit, we must repent of our wrongs, and God will help us. He only wants our good, and repentance of sin is good. Yes, it can be painful to admit our shortcomings and wrong doings, but it is also freeing. Sin causes us to want to live in the dark, where our wrongs are not seen. In Ephesians we are reminded that God calls us into the light, where we can see our sin and ask for forgiveness. As Christians, we desire to live in the light of the Lord where goodness, righteousness, and truth are produced.

There is a great example of kindness in John's Gospel. In the miracle of the multiplication of the loaves and fish (John 6:1–15), we focus, correctly, on it as a prefiguring of the Eucharist. And it is. But before Jesus gets the bread and fish, the food is in the possession of a boy. This boy, because he is good and kind, gives what he has to Jesus. And Jesus does with the bread and the fish the same thing that he does with everything we give him. He makes more—so much more that there is enough for five thousand men, plus an unknown number of women and children, with leftovers that fill twelve baskets! That boy's small kindness helped many people.

Even in popular culture, the idea of goodness and kindness are extolled. The movie *Pay it Forward* was about a teacher who asked her students to do three random acts of kindness, and to ask the recipients of their kindness to do the same for others. The concept of random acts of kindness has become a movement now, celebrated on the Friday after Thanksgiving and for a week in February.

Thankfully, God offers us acts of goodness and kindness every day. And we are called to do the same. In Matthew 18:21–35, Jesus teaches us that forgiveness is a kindness given to us by God, and we are to give it to others. A king, "moved with compassion," forgives a servant's debt. The servant, then, goes out and sees a person who owes him a debt, but he chooses to not show the same kindness as was shown to him. The king finds out and has the servant thrown into prison and tortured. Jesus concludes the parable by saying, "So will my heavenly Father do to you, unless each of you forgives his brother from his heart" (Matthew 18:35). It is our Christian duty to treat each other with goodness and kindness.

An Invitation to Share

1. Do kindness and goodness seem attainable in our times? Or are these fruits going to cause us to be taken of advantage of and to be thought of as naive?

_____

_____

_____

_____

_____

_____

_____

_____

_____

_____

_____

_____

_____

_____

2. In Micah 6:8, it says, "You have been told, O mortal, what is good, and what the LORD requires of you: Only to do justice and to love goodness, and to walk humbly with your God." How do you see Jesus' words in Matthew 5:38–42 connected to what God told the people of Israel in Micah?

_____

_____

_____

_____

_____

_____

_____

_____

_____

_____

_____

_____

_____

3. What do those two passages from Micah and Matthew look like today, in your particular set of life circumstances? Is the Spirit moving you to do more in this area of your life?

_____

_____

_____

_____

_____

_____

_____

_____

_____

_____

_____

_____

_____

_____

_____

_____

_____

_____

Closing Prayer

Father, you have given me so many examples of goodness and kindness in your words and actions. You have reached out to me and shown me your goodness and kindness always, even when I do not deserve it. Scripture is full of all the ways you have showered me with your blessings. My life is filled with joy because of you. All of this you do out of love for me, and, in turn, you ask me to do the same for others. It is not easy, Father, to be good and kind in the world today, but it is necessary. My desire is to share what you have given me with others, because I know that each small act of goodness and kindness can show your love and can serve as an example to others. Following you means I am called to be a light in the world, a light which shines with goodness and kindness. May the Holy Spirit fill me with what I need to be the light in my corner of the world. I ask all of this in Jesus' name. Amen.

Kindness and Goodness

6: Self-Control and Gentleness

Opening Prayer

Lord, you have given us free will, but because our first parents, Adam and Eve, abused that free will, we all now suffer. You have also given me the means to be responsible, but I often fail and wonder why you gave us a free will, which seems to cost so very much. I, like so many others, struggle with gaining control over bad habits or addictions; I have watched people I love be lured into addiction, and I have seen the hurt and devastation it causes. I need to rely on your strength and power, Lord, not my own, to overcome my failings. You alone can help me live a life free in your love and grace.

You call me to freedom through the love of you, love of self, and love of neighbor. It is in accepting your love, so freely given, that I can have control and move toward being gentle of spirit. Rooted in your love, I find hope. Send me your Holy Spirit to remind me to turn to you, to seek your face, and to give you the control so that I may live in you and for you. I am grateful for all that you have done and continue to do in my life. I give you thanks and glory, always.

Amen.

Self-Control
Gentleness

On My Heart

Cultivate Self-Control and Gentleness with the Holy Spirit

Self-control sounds almost as difficult as willpower. And that first part of the word, "self," seems to indicate that we must rely on ourselves to have it. If you have ever been on a diet or have had to exclude certain foods or drinks you enjoy for health reasons, you know that it's not easy to exercise self-control. We live in a world that seems to believe self-control is for other people. Freedom to do what I want, when I want, and how I want is the name of the game. There is little to recommend in that thought pattern; it is selfish and not for those who believe we are made in God's image.

How often have you thought that someone needs some self-control? Have you ever thought about your own lack of control in certain areas? For some, our mouth is a problem. We have trouble controlling our urge to express everything. Even in prayer, we cannot just say "Please pray for Sue, who is having a difficult pregnancy." We add information about her husband, her job, and her great aunt! I was once guilty of that until I heard it referred to as "holy gossip." Gossip is never holy, even if couched in a prayer request. Now, when people start to overshare, I remind them that God knows the details, so we do not need to hear them.

Some folks lie about themselves and others, possibly to look better than they are or, sadly, maybe out of jealousy. It is hurtful when gossip, true or untrue, is spread in a community.

Where Do You Need Self-Control?

Food can be a source of lack of control for many of us. Sirach 37:27–31 has this to say about food:

> My son, while you are well, govern your appetite, and see that you do not allow it what is bad for you. For not everything is good for everyone, nor is everything suited to every taste. Do not go to excess with any enjoyment, neither become a glutton for choice foods; For sickness comes with overeating, and gluttony brings on nausea. Through lack of self-control many have died, but the abstemious one prolongs life.

Food is my biggest weakness. It has been a problem from my teens until now. I cannot say I have overcome the problem, though I have identified some root causes. I like to eat well. If you came to dinner, you would enjoy all fresh, homemade items. You might wonder how a person who cooks such healthy, yet tasty, food is overweight. While I know what foods to eat to feel my best and stay healthy, I repeatedly succumb to food that does not serve me well. When I am sad or lonely or angry or frustrated or tired, I eat as a way of avoiding the real problem or emotion.

Not everyone turns to food in times of pain. Some turn to shopping, gambling, escaping by reading, becoming obsessive about prayer or exercise, or drinking. (Please note, I am speaking here about coping mechanisms; when the coping mechanism does not allow a person to function in her life, when it has become an addiction, professional help may be needed.) What in your life are you allowing to control you instead of you exercising self-control over it?

Other people may have a bad temper: and, again, I'm raising my hand here. This one is tricky because sometimes people really do make a mistake or hurt you or want to cause problems for you. However, while we cannot control how others treat us, we can control how we react. We are called to gentleness, to have gentle spirits, showing care and concern with love, not with force.

Passion or Problem?

We need self-control. In my experience, most people have one or two areas where self-control can be a problem. Sirach 18:30–33 has this to say, "Do not let your passions be your guide, but keep your desires in check. If you allow yourself to satisfy your passions, they will make you the laughingstock of your enemies. Take no pleasure in too much luxury which brings on poverty redoubled. Do not become a glutton and a drunkard with nothing in your purse."

We cannot allow our passions to control us, or we will become a laughingstock to our enemies, and not to argue with Sirach, but maybe to our friends as well. Too much of anything is not good for us, be it hard on our wallet, our family, our waistline, our time, or our future. Sirach is not saying that passion is a bad thing. Passion can drive us to good if we put God and those he has given to us before our passion. But passion is not good if we strive for what we love to the exclusion of God and others. And it can happen. Passion must be tempered and controlled, or it will overtake us. Another way to look at it is to ask what is our motivation in this situation? Am I going to the gym to be healthy and strong or to show off how good I look? If I buy new clothes, am I taking money away from something my family needs? Letting our passions rule us can lead to problems.

In Chapter 3 on patience, I mentioned the practice of pause and pray. It is equally as effective for self-control as it is for patience. When faced with a problem, an overwhelming emotion, or a difficult situation, take a moment to pause. What do you really need at this moment of emotional or physical pain? It always helps me to "offer it up" or turn it over to God as an offering for someone else who needs relief or for the souls in purgatory. I pray for a solution, trying to do the right thing instead of the easy thing or the thing I want. Each of us has different solutions. For me, coffee helps when I'm craving food. If I am angry, removing myself from the situation and getting some physical activity is helpful. Eventually, with prayer and practice, you will gain better self-control.

Stand in the truth that inside of you is a spirit of self-control that we can access by asking God to bring it forth and by relying on him to provide us with the means to resist whatever we need to resist. It is not in our power, but in his, that we can pass up the chocolate cake or drink or shoes that we do not need or cannot afford.

Gentleness

When looking up gentleness in Scripture, it is often paired with instructions for correction and defending the faith. Interestingly, both St. Paul and St. Peter urge correction with gentleness. In 1 Corinthians 4:21, Paul asks, "Which do you prefer? Shall I come to you with a rod, or with love and a gentle spirit?" St. Peter reminds us to "Always be ready to give an explanation to anyone who asks you for a reason for your hope, but do it with gentleness and reverence, keeping your conscience clear, so that, when you are maligned, those who defame your good conduct in Christ may themselves be put to shame" (1 Peter 3:15–16).

At one time or another, many of us have found ourselves in need of correcting or disciplining someone. From children to employees to family members and friends, we may have found ourselves in a situation where correction is necessary. As is often the case, we have been told to do it with gentleness, especially in matters of the faith. It is not always easy to do this, but looking at Jesus' example in the Gospels can help us. The story of the woman caught in adultery (John 8:1–11) is one that shows us how gentle Jesus was in the face of a difficult situation. You can almost feel how angry the crowd is and how intense their desire is to "get" both Jesus and the woman. But Jesus does not give in to their loud cries and demands. Instead, he is quiet and still. Is he reflecting on the problem, or does he already have a plan in mind? Either way, his attitude disarms the crowd and the woman. Jesus speaks with love; he speaks with gentleness, and the woman knows she is safe—not only from the threat of stoning, but safe with this man, with Jesus. In the last verse of the passage, Jesus says, "Neither do I condemn you. Go, [and] from now on do not sin any more" (John 8:11). Are we that gentle when we correct others? Or do we go over all the times the person was wrong before, mocking their attempts to change and calling attention to the sin in a way that embarrasses and belittles them? Jesus does not go into a discourse about why the woman sinned or how awful she is as a person. We can strive to do the same. We can learn to use our self-control and be gentle when correcting others.

What do we want people to know about us? We want them to know that they are safe with us, that we want only their good, and that the correction is meant out of love and concern. People can accept or reject what we tell them, but if the manner in which we behave is canceling out the message, we need to consider changing our behavior.

Image of Gentleness

When I think of an image of Jesus that embodies gentleness it is that of the Good Shepherd, gently placing the wayward lamb on his shoulder and bringing it back to the flock, where it belongs. Jesus tells the people gathered, in Luke 15:4–5, "What man among you having a hundred sheep and losing one of them would not leave the ninety-nine in the desert and go after the lost one until he finds it? And when he does find it, he sets it on his shoulders with great joy." He is happy to have found the lost sheep and to be bringing it back to the flock. Now, as lay people, we cannot literally bring others back into the flock since we cannot hear confession and offer absolution, which only a priest can do. What we can do is correct gently, with love, and hope that the person goes to Confession if necessary.

When we look at self-control, we can see how having more of it can lead to a gentleness of spirit. Taking the time and effort to gain control over our needs and emotions helps us to cultivate gentleness. That gentleness can begin with how we treat ourselves and then move to how we treat others. One reason self-control and gentleness fit together for me is that I spent much of my life with harsh exterior and then interior means of control. I was—well, in honesty, I often still am—very hard on myself. I have grown to be less harsh with others. I found it did more harm than good, and now I work from the premise that gentleness in word and deed is better both for me and for those I want to teach, serve, or influence.

An Invitation to Ponder

What do self-control and gentleness mean to you? Do you recognize that God treats you with gentleness, or do you need constant reminders? Do you consider yourself to be in possession of these fruits of the Spirit when dealing with yourself or others?

_____

_____

_____

_____

_____

_____

_____

_____

_____

_____

_____

_____

_____

_____

_____

Connecting to Scripture

PRAYER BEFORE READING SCRIPTURE

Father, fill me with the Holy Spirit to guide me as I read and reflect on your Word. I ask for the grace to allow your Word to flood my soul that I may grow ever closer to you and your Son Jesus. Amen.

⟋ Proverbs 18:6-9 _____

_____

_____

⟋ Proverbs 25:28 and 29:11 _____

_____

_____

⟋ Sirach 21:11 _____

_____

_____

⟋ 2 Timothy 1:7 _____

_____

_____

✐ 1 Peter 3:4 _____

_____

_____

Scripture Reflection

If we want to be good Christians, having self-control seems non-negotiable. The good news? Scripture is straightforward in telling us what will happen if we lack control. Proverbs 18:6–9 tells us to think before we speak and not to lie. If we do not watch our tongue, we will have fights and trouble, and be foolish and defenseless. I am sure many of us have said things we regret. Sometimes it is in the heat of an argument or tense situation. Other times it might be a quick response to a text or phone call. I am very guilty of the quick response under the guise of resolving things quickly even though it is not always necessary or advisable to do so. Waiting for more information or for emotions to settle is a better solution and helps me to have fewer regrets. Asking the Holy Spirit for guidance before responding is the way I have learned (though not perfectly) to not rush in speaking.

In Sirach 21:11 we are told to know and keep the Law, to control our thoughts, and to have "fear of the Lord." It makes sense; if we know what God wants from us (the Law), then we are in a better position to do what is right. Besides knowing and keeping the law, we have Christ, who died for us. Before he left this earth, he gave his apostles the gift of peace, which has been passed on to us as well. Colossians 3:15 says, "Let the peace of Christ control your hearts, the peace into which you were called in one body. And be thankful." This shows us that while the standard of what God wants from us may seem high, he, certainly, gives us what we need to meet that standard.

Each of us, as children of God, has within ourselves the ability to have self-control because of what God has given us (2 Timothy 1:7). It's in our soul, in our being, a part of us that God wants us to use. We have a "spirit of power and love and self-control" from God through the outpouring of the Holy Spirit.

Do you ever think about how God sees you, or how he will see you when you die? When I start to think about it, I start with my list of all the things that are not right, not good, and not holy. Much of what I think about is external, at least initially. Then I remember that God sees past all the externals to the internal, to my soul. And in there, my desire is for an imperishable beauty, which is dependent not on our exterior looks but on our "hidden character, expressed ... in a gentle and calm disposition." That disposition is "precious in the sight of God" (1 Peter 3:4). Do you want to be precious in God's sight?

An Invitation to Share

1. Which stories from the Gospels would you use as examples of times when Jesus modeled self-control and gentleness for us? Which examples do you think are the hardest to emulate? Which do you believe are easier?

_____

_____

_____

_____

_____

_____

_____

_____

_____

_____

_____

_____

_____

2. In what ways does your disposition need to change or improve?
   Think of at least two concrete steps you can take that will help you
   begin to make those changes today.

_____

_____

_____

_____

_____

_____

_____

_____

_____

_____

_____

3. Which is more difficult for you, self-control or gentleness? What concrete steps can you take to grow in your area of greatest need?

_____

_____

_____

_____

_____

_____

_____

_____

_____

_____

_____

_____

_____

_____

_____

_____

_____

_____

_____

_____

Closing Prayer

Father God, self-control is very difficult at times, especially when so many things do not seem to go my way, and I use other things to comfort and console myself. Sometimes I want to control everything and everyone except myself, and I know this is wrong. Help me to turn to you when I get angry or feel overwhelmed with life. Lead me to gentleness, especially with those people over whom I have authority.

Holy Spirit, fill me with the fruits of self-control and gentleness so I can overcome selfish tendencies and unhealthy desires with your help and guidance. I believe this is possible when I remain close to you in your Word, in prayer, and in the sacraments. Remind me to do that, Lord, so that I stay away from things that cause me pain and embrace things that help me. Thank you for all you have done for me and all you continue to do.

May I follow your example of self-control and gentleness always.

Amen.

Self-Control and Gentleness

7: Love

Opening Prayer

Love, Lord, is what we all seek. We might even think we can earn it, but we cannot. Your love is our ultimate example of what is true and perfect. Thank you for the love you have shown me in creating me, in giving your Son to me, and in sending your Holy Spirit to me. You are selfless, only wanting my good. That is the love that I need and that this world needs—a love where the other is put first. Teach me to have a love that seeks the good of others and does not look for a reward. Fill me with love like yours, and then I ask for the courage to share it with others—not only with those whom I know and love but also with those who are difficult to love. I ask for the grace to bring love to all those who come into my life. The fruit of a life spent in service to others is love; guide me, Holy Spirit, to be of service to those in need. I ask for all of this, trusting in your love, through your Son and the Spirit.

Amen.

On My Heart

_____

_____

_____

_____

_____

_____

_____

_____

_____

_____

_____

_____

_____

_____

Cultivate Love with the Holy Spirit

The first fruit of the Spirit in Galatians mentioned by St. Paul is love. So why is love the last chapter of this study? It is the fruit that is most evident in our lives when we have all the other fruits. You might call it the capstone or the fruit that encompasses all the other fruits. St. Paul writes about love in a few of his letters. Many of us are probably familiar with his verses in 1 Corinthians 13, particularly verses 4–7:

> Love is patient, love is kind. It is not jealous, [love] is not pomp-
> ous, it is not inflated, it is not rude, it does not seek its own in-

terests, it is not quick-tempered, it does not brood over injury, it does not rejoice over wrongdoing but rejoices with the truth. It bears all things, believes all things, hopes all things, endures all things.

If you have been to a Catholic wedding in the last twenty years, you've probably heard it. This verse, therefore, is often associated with romantic love, for what is more romantic than a wedding? Of course, married folks know that love is not so much romantic as it is self-sacrificing.

Another problem with the word "love" in English is that we refer to our love for everything and everyone with the same word. Do we really love pizza, coffee, and dogs in the same way we love our best friend, spouse, and children. Now I enjoy good coffee, but I do not love it in the same way that I love my husband!

In Scripture, it is almost always agape love, which is held up and spoken of, and which is neither a romantic, fuzzy feeling nor would it be depicted by two people running towards each other in a meadow of daisies. Agape love is a self-giving, lay-down-one's-life kind of love. It is the love God has for us and the love we strive to have for him and one another.

The Catechism quotes St. Thomas Aquinas' definition of the highest form of love: "to will the good of the other" (*Catechism*, 1766). Clearly, that is the fruit of the Spirit that we want. We want to be able to do as Jesus entreats, "But I say to you, love your enemies, and pray for those who persecute you, that you may be children of your heavenly Father" (Matthew 5:44–45a). These verses tell us how much God loves us: "But God proves his love for us in that while we were still sinners Christ died for us" (Romans 5:8), and "See what love the Father has bestowed on us that we may be called the children of God"

(1 John 3:1). It is through the gift of Jesus' death that we are truly God's children; he allowed the sacrifice of his Son so that we could become his daughters and sons.

God's Love

When I was young, I believed, probably like many people, that God showed his love to me by keeping me from harm, making sure good things happened to me, and pretty much making things go my way. Sure, I had to keep up my end of the bargain and thought I did a fine job. I went to Mass every Sunday, volunteered in Church, usually obeyed my parents, and although I did fight with my siblings, they were so annoying that I felt justified.

As I grew up, my idea of God as Santa Claus changed into an image of him as a judge, who was always watching me—not in a benevolent, loving way, but because he wanted to catch me doing the wrong thing. As I entered my teenage and high school years and as my idea of who I was developed, my concept of who God was changed again. I realized I was separate from my parents and family, and while they were a big influence, God could be an influence as well.

God became that wise, old man, complete with a white beard, smiling down on all of us, shaking his head in wonder as we made mistakes, and patiently waiting for us to find our way back to him. In high school, I went on a retreat called Christian Awakening. On this weekend the primary focus was to help us know—not just in our head but in our soul—that God loved us, that we were good, that he made us, and that he gave us his Son out of the perfect love he has for each one of us. I still recall the phrase we learned that weekend, "God don't make junk." I know, it's not quite correct in the grammar department, but it was a much-needed message for me as someone who often felt like I was not quite as good as everyone else.

As teens, many of us struggle with believing we are lovable. We fight with ourselves and believe we are not good enough, so we wonder how God can love us. For me, the proof is—Jesus. On that weekend, I learned that even if the world were against me, it would somehow work out because "if God is for us, who can be against us?" (Romans 8:31) And if I had any further doubts, he gave us his only begotten Son even if we did not quite deserve it.

As we mature from teens to young adults to adults, we begin to better understand what agape is about. Often this knowledge comes out of a struggle between you and another person. For me, it is my husband who taught me what it means to love someone the way God does.

Loving Others

I have been married a long time, and I married quite young. I loved my husband when I married him, but really had no idea what that meant. My head and heart were expecting an idealized version of fairy tale love and romance with no troubles. I quickly learned that was not the case. To learn how to become one with my husband, there were many trials and struggles, mainly because neither of us knew what we were doing. After many years, we stopped fighting about who was right and started to think about what was best for our family. This requires much self-emptying on everyone's part, and it is not easy.

After thirty years of marriage, we celebrated with a wonderful trip to Italy. And when we returned home, we faced anew what it meant to love each other. My husband was hospitalized for twelve days, underwent five different procedures, including one surgery, and then had to go for hyperbaric treatments. I had to learn how to change dressings, flush a PICC (peripherally inserted central catheter) line, and change the continuous IV (intravenous) bag of antibiotics. He had to take a leave of absence from work, and he couldn't drive because he was wearing a boot on his right foot. It was a difficult time.

I hoped and prayed that that the cause of these problems would never repeat itself and that my husband would take more responsibility for his health. For a time, he did, and life returned to our normal. Unfortunately, that healthy state did not last as long as I had hoped, and we, once again, found ourselves dealing with serious health problems.

I could not understand why this was happening again. How many times does a man need to suffer to learn a lesson? I was furious—so much so that all I could think about was protecting myself and not helping my husband at all. I kept praying and praying, railing at God, demanding that he do something to show my husband that I was right in my desire to step away, rather than toward, my husband in his time of need.

My desire to protect myself was rooted in fear and anger, not in love. I wanted to protect myself from getting hurt, and my plan was to withdraw my support. After all, it was not my fault my husband was having problems again. I wanted God to affirm my decision to not support my husband in his recovery because I believed God would want me to protect myself.

One day, while in the car, after having been to spiritual direction and having spent time praying in the chapel of the retreat center, I was again begging God to tell me what to do so I could protect myself. And I heard in my heart, "There is no protecting yourself. You need to be all in." That was not what I wanted to hear at all. I stopped and went for a walk to think about this "all in" business. You know that feeling you have, deep in your soul, when you realize that God is trying very hard to teach you something. Once I realized what God was teaching me, I thought, "This really shouldn't be such a shock; I really should have known this."

God reminded me that Jesus was "all in" to the point of dying for us. I did not need to die for my husband to show my love to him; I needed to die to myself and love as Jesus did. As it says in John 12:24, "Unless a grain of wheat falls to the ground and dies, it remains just a grain of wheat; but if it dies, it produces much fruit." It is love that gives us the strength to die to what we want in order to do what is good, right, and just. When we die to our selfishness, we can produce fruit. If I have learned anything in my life as a wife, mother, daughter, sister, and friend it is that dying to self always brings a great return of love into my life.

There is another side of the story about my husband, John, and learning to love. It is the love he has shown to me and our children in our life together. First, he rarely says no to me. Every idea I have of things I want to do, recipes to try, places to go, even the opera, he tries all of it for me. And if I cook something he's not crazy about, he eats it anyway and then says, "Honey, you don't need to make that again."

When our children were young he was the at-home parent. Sometimes people commented on how nice it was to see a dad "babysitting" his kids; John would reply he didn't consider caring for his children to be babysitting; he considered it just being a dad. He took our daughter to get her ears pierced and learned to braid her hair. When our son was a scout, John helped at den meetings and organized popcorn sales. When I traveled for work, I knew the kids had home cooked meals and clean clothes to wear because John made it happen. In our family, there is none of this "It's not my job," well, except for me—I don't take out the trash or mow the lawn.

Joking aside, my marriage is not perfect, and there are times when tempers flare and voices are raised. In truth, it's usually my temper and my voice. But, ultimately, it is love that brings us back together and smooths out the problems.

An Invitation to Ponder

When is it difficult to love someone the way you know you are being called to love him or her? Does the thought of emptying yourself give you strength or frighten you?

_____

_____

_____

_____

_____

_____

_____

_____

_____

_____

_____

_____

_____

_____

_____

_____

_____

_____

Connecting to Scripture

PRAYER BEFORE READING SCRIPTURE

Father, fill me with the Holy Spirit to guide me as I read and reflect on your Word. I ask for the grace to allow your Word to flood my soul that I may grow ever closer to you and your Son Jesus. Amen.

☞ Deuteronomy 6:5 _____

_____

_____

☞ Hosea 6:6 _____

_____

_____

☞ John 3:16 _____

_____

_____

☞ Romans 12:9–21 _____

_____

_____

9 1 John 4:7 _____

_____

_____

Scripture Reflection

Right in the beginning of God calling the Israelites to himself, there is love. He says, "You shall love the LORD, your God, with your whole heart, and with your whole being, and with your whole strength" (Deuteronomy 6:5). He is clear: whole heart, whole being, whole strength. There is no half, no partial loving of God. You are either in or out. What goes along with loving God? In Hosea, we see that God desires our loyalty and that we have knowledge of him. He is not looking for blind obedience. He is looking for us to know about him so that we freely choose to love.

Why does God desire this freely chosen and total love? Because he knows that loving him will provide us with what we need to have an abundant life and that we will gain eternal life, as we are reminded in John 3:16. It is not a bad deal, is it?

I am going to make a radical suggestion now. As I read Romans 12:9–13, I realized that those verses speak very specifically about how to treat others, even to the point of telling us how we can conquer evil. What is the radical suggestion? Let that passage be the one that comes to mind when we think of love, instead of the passage from 1 Corinthians 13:1–13, which I mentioned at the beginning of this chapter.

Romans reminds us of how to behave. We are to love and honor each other, be fervent, serve God, rejoice, hope, endure troubles, pray always, share with others, regard everyone as equals, bless our enemies, seek peace, do not look for revenge, and conquer evil with good. This is the love God wants us to have for each other. Romans gives us a roadmap with specific instructions to follow.

How do we know if we love someone enough? In a sense, there is no "enough" in love. Thomas Merton says this about love: "Love seeks one thing only. The good of the one loved. It leaves all the other secondary effects to take care of themselves. Love, therefore, is its own reward."[4] That is our answer to the question of whether we are loving enough. Are we seeking the good of the one we love?

Remember, we are not speaking here of romantic love. We are speaking here of the love we have for each other as human persons. The love that seeks the good of the other is the basis for all relationships we have in our lives. We are called to love each other in an agape way. We cannot have deep, meaningful relationships with others if we do not want their good above our own. I go back to the idea of self-emptying. If we are full of ourselves, there is no room for what God, through the Holy Spirit, wants to give us. When we are empty, we can be filled with the fruits of the Holy Spirit and share them with the people God puts in our lives.

All of us have been shown love by God in a very telling way; he gave us his Son, who died for us. We are also called to love as Jesus did—maybe not to the point of dying, but certainly to the point of giving ourselves to others. In John 3:16, we read, "For God so loved the world that he gave his only Son, so that everyone who believes in him might not perish but might have eternal life." God's love is the gift of salvation, given to us through Jesus.

Hopefully throughout this study we have grown in our knowledge and understanding of the fruits of the Spirit. We have moved closer to God and can better appreciate St. John the Evangelist's words from his first letter. We come from God, and when we love as he does, we know him. But we must take to heart and live out the first words of the verse, "Beloved, let us love one another" (1 John 4:7); this is how we will change ourselves, our families, and our world.

An Invitation to Share

1. How can we, as women, impart this agape love to others?

_____

_____

_____

_____

_____

_____

_____

_____

_____

_____

_____

2. When is it difficult to give yourself to others, to love them selflessly?

_____

_____

_____

_____

_____

_____

_____

_____

_____

_____

3. Besides loving the people in our life, we love God. How does loving God help you to love others?

_____

_____

_____

_____

_____

_____

_____

_____

_____

_____

_____

_____

_____

_____

_____

_____

_____

4. Years ago, there was a song with the words "and they'll know we are Christians by our love." Can that be said of you?

_____

_____

_____

_____

_____

_____

_____

_____

_____

_____

_____

_____

Closing Prayer

Dear God, you love me so much that you created me in your image. And then you gave me the gift of salvation by sending your Son Jesus, who died for me. All of Scripture points to your love for all of us as a people and for me as one person. I am your daughter, who longs to be filled with your love. You have shown me what love is by your action in my life. Time and time again you have loved me from brokenness to healing and wholeness. For this I am grateful; your love compels me to share the love with others in this world—my family, friends, neighbors, and those in need. Help me to love my enemies and those whom I do not understand. Allow the Holy Spirit to fill me with love that overflows to others, heals others, and conquers evil. Let love replace fear. I ask all this in Jesus' name.

Amen.

Endnotes

1   Mother Teresa of Calcutta, *Seeking the Heart of God: Reflections on Prayer*, (San Francisco: HarperOne, 1993).

2   For more information on the other titles available in the *Stay Connected* series visit www.gracewatch.media.

3   "Prayer of Saint Teresa of Avila." EWTN.com. https://www.ewtn.com/devotionals/prayers/StTeresaofAvila.htm/ (accessed on May 15, 2018).

4   Thomas Merton, *No Man Is an Island,* (New York City: Image Doubleday, 1967).